Spectacular Key West

Landscapes, Sunsets, and Architecture

Vaughn Garner

Spectacular Key West
by Vaughn Garner

For information please go to: www.vaughngarnerphotography.com

ISBN 978-0-9886257-1-6

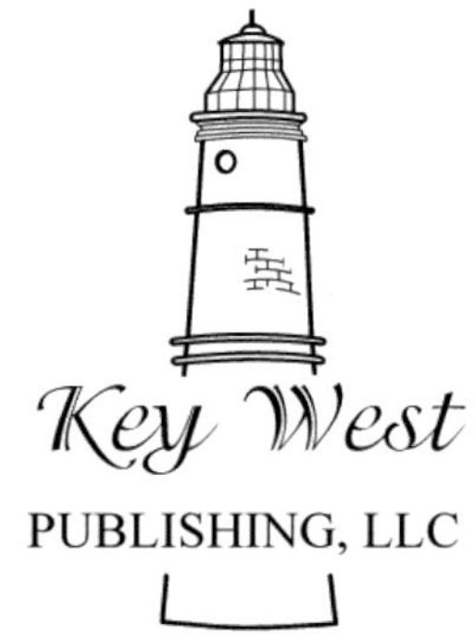

Printed in USA
CPSIA: 1-2000-13-21932

Acknowledgements

I'd like to acknowledge the help, encouragement and unwavering support of Karen Beauprie, Bob Bernreuter, Heather Boettcher, Kristin Brent, Veronica Brown, Coral Walker-Cinco, Vicki Clark, Joyce Dahlberg, Fran Decker, Tommy DeFrancesco, Eric Dehn, Dallas Doctor, Suzanne Egle, Jon Emig, Captain Glenn A. Evans Jr., Layne Garner, Tiffany Garner, Todd Garner, Caralyn Gilliland, George Gilliland, Susan Hamilton, TC Hanke, Nadja Hansen, Barbara Hayo, Ellen Herbert, Michael Jordan, John Kelley, Kayla Kelley, Sonja Kelley, Stephen Kelley, Ed Krane, Dee Long, Kelly Maatta, Christian Marabona, Stormy McCall, Valeria McCall, William McIntyre, Stephanie Montesino, Rachel Morrow, Jeanea Neugebauer, Tammy Osterhoudt, Judy Owens, Ben Phillips, Frank Porter, Taylor Sanderson, Marty Shoeneman, Gail Sibley, Eduardo Silva, Jenna Stauffer, Ed Swift III, Laurie Turk, Karen Walker, BJ Andrade-Ward, and Robert Wright.

A very special thank you to Eva Conaway, Mary Martinez, and Linda Test.

This book is dedicated to my parents,
Bert and Carma Garner, who first taught me to appreciate the wonders of nature.

About the Author

Three years in the making, *Spectacular Key West* includes 74 stunning photographs. It is my tribute to Key West, after living here for ten years. Moving to Key West is one of the best decisions I have ever made and the island city permanently changed my outlook on life. When I first arrived in this tropical paradise, sans suit and tie, my goal was to party and hang out at the beach. Little did I know that moving here would lead me to a pinnacle of my professional life. Key West has taught me to slow down and appreciate the historic architecture and natural wonders surrounding me. This book conveys the experience, by sharing landscapes, sunrises and sunsets, as well as the best of Key West's famous 19th Century architecture.

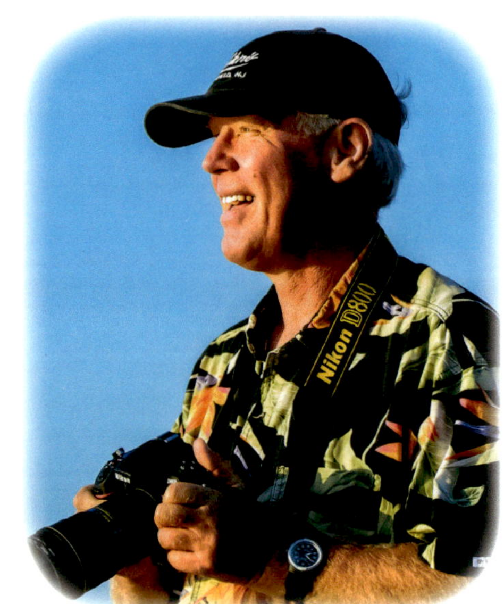

Photo courtesy of Veronica Brown.

"I first met Vaughn in 2011 and I think it is true to say that when he spoke with me about showing his photographs in SoDu Gallery, I immediately felt both his joy and passion for Key West. Since that time, Vaughn has developed his art into a style all his own. He has learned to capture the essence of the nature that surrounds and envelops our little island. It is Vaughn Garner's imagination and creativity that makes his photographs in *Spectacular Key West* come alive and are an inspiration, forever reminding us of how lucky we are to live on a tropical island."

Karen Beauprie - Artist, owner and partner, SoDu Gallery, Key West.

On August 10, 2010 Vaughn received the "Award of Merit" from the New York Institute of Photography, for "*Cloud Sails*."

On December 20, 2011 Vaughn graduated from the New York Institute of Photography.

The Theatre of Morning

It's still dark. I'm sitting on the beach and the sand is cool and slightly damp on my feet. I feel a wayward ant crawl up my calf and I brush it away. A crescent moon is slowly leaving the scene in preparation for the main event. The sky is turning in ombré shades from black to deep blue, as the stars start to vanish, one by one.

The air has the tropical heaviness that is Key West, but this morning, it's not that humid. It's quiet and still. There are no cars coming around the bend on South Roosevelt. Occasionally I hear a jogger go by on the sidewalk, the only indication that I'm not completely alone with nature.

There's almost no wind, rare for early October. In the distance, the top of the palms are still. A few puffy clouds dot the sky close to the horizon. The ocean is as smooth as glass. I smile. I've been waiting for a morning like this for many days.

Colors start to appear at the horizon, as the restless sun discovers the clouds. Spectacular!

Photography is the art of communicating emotion - sharing the actual feeling of seeing the wonderful beauty of nature. Photography means, literally, "writing with light." Key West, because of its geographical location, has very unique light. This light sets the stage for the day in exceptional, spectacular fashion.

Key West will always hold a special place in my heart. I have never ceased to love it, to enjoy living beneath the sunlight of enthralling days in Cayo Hueso.

As you turn the pages, immerse yourself in the unique beauty of the Florida Keys' landscapes, sunsets and architecture. Bring back fond memories of Key West by exploring the nuances of each photograph. Be inspired by stunning works that have been described as both surreal and impressionistic.

Enjoy!

Vaughn Garner

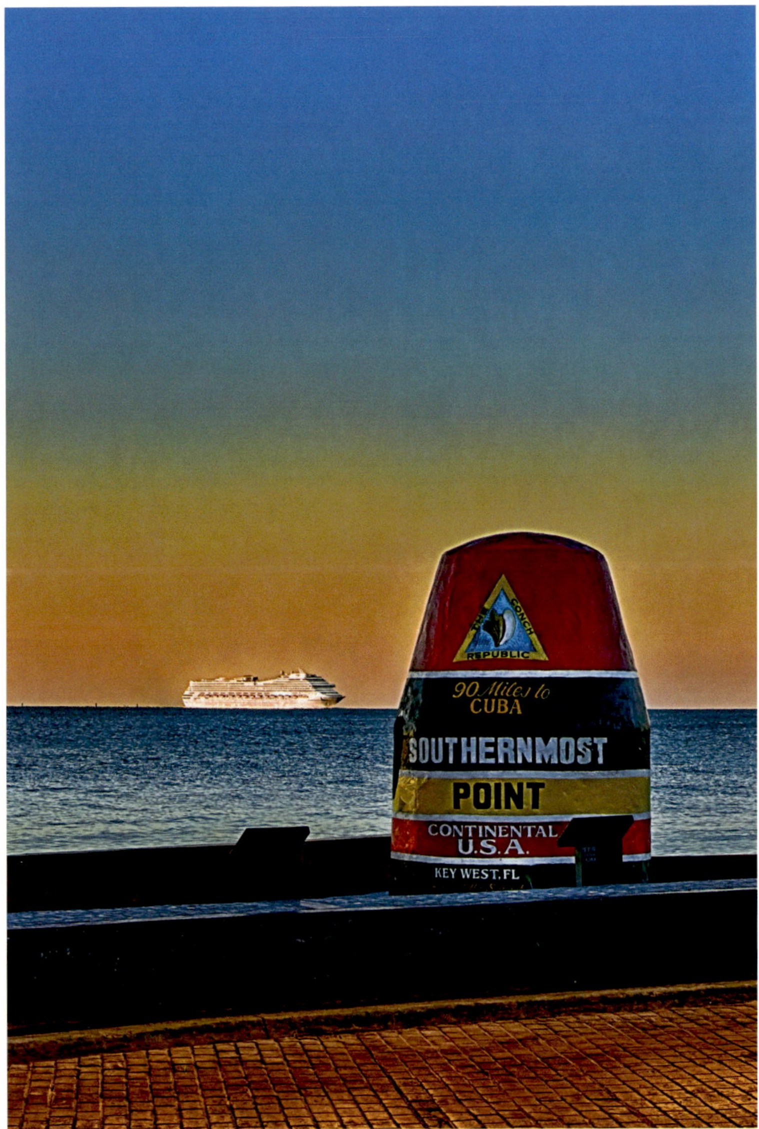

Southernmost Point: Welcome to Key West! You are now at the southernmost point in the southernmost city in the continental United States. 90 miles from Cuba and 157 miles from Miami, there's no place on the planet quite like Key West! Enjoy our tropical island city.

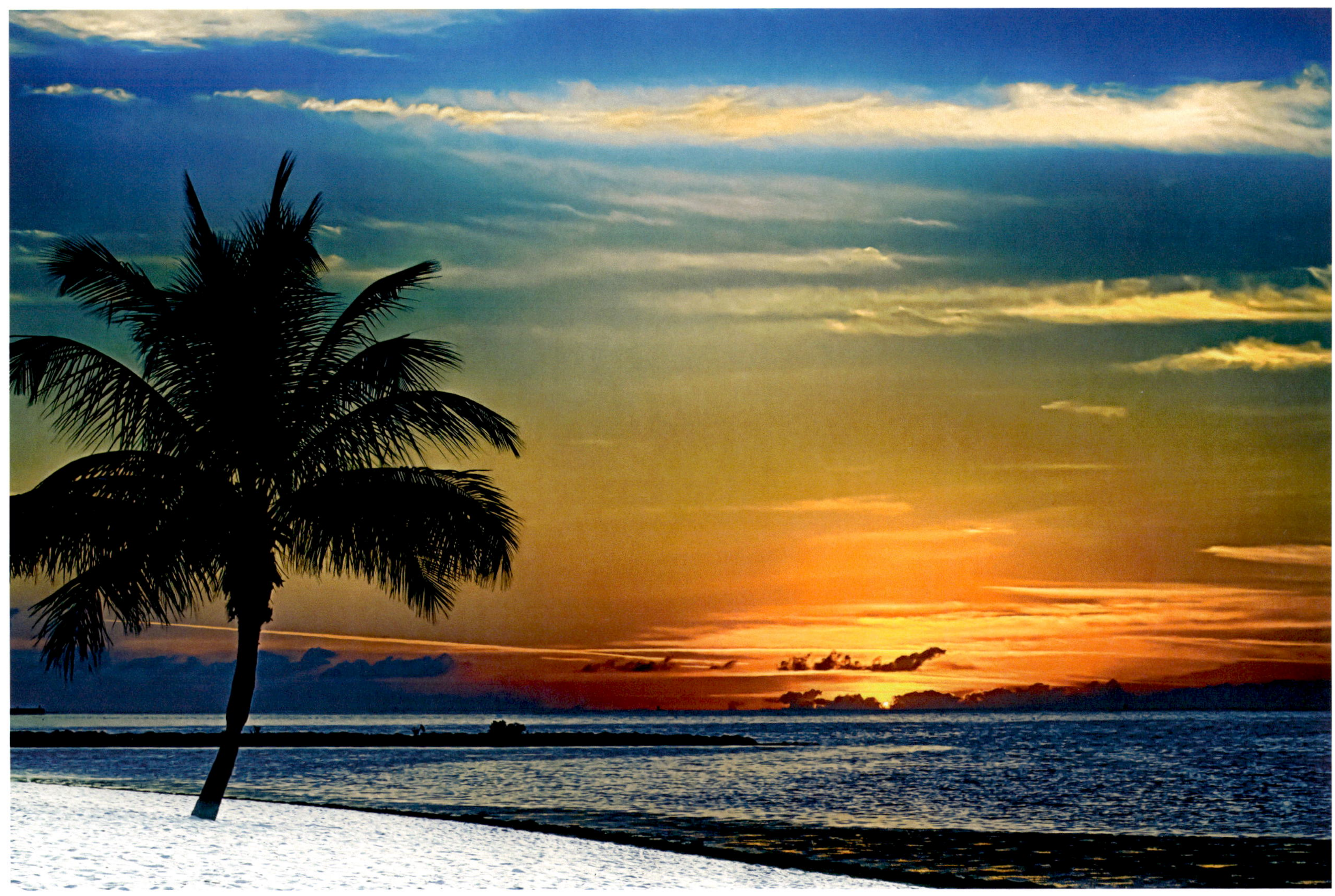

KeyWest Magical Sunrise: The sun has yet to rise, but shines brightly on the clouds at the top. The clouds at the horizon are perfect, the colors magnificent! Each sunrise is unique and this one shows how serene a Key West morning can be.

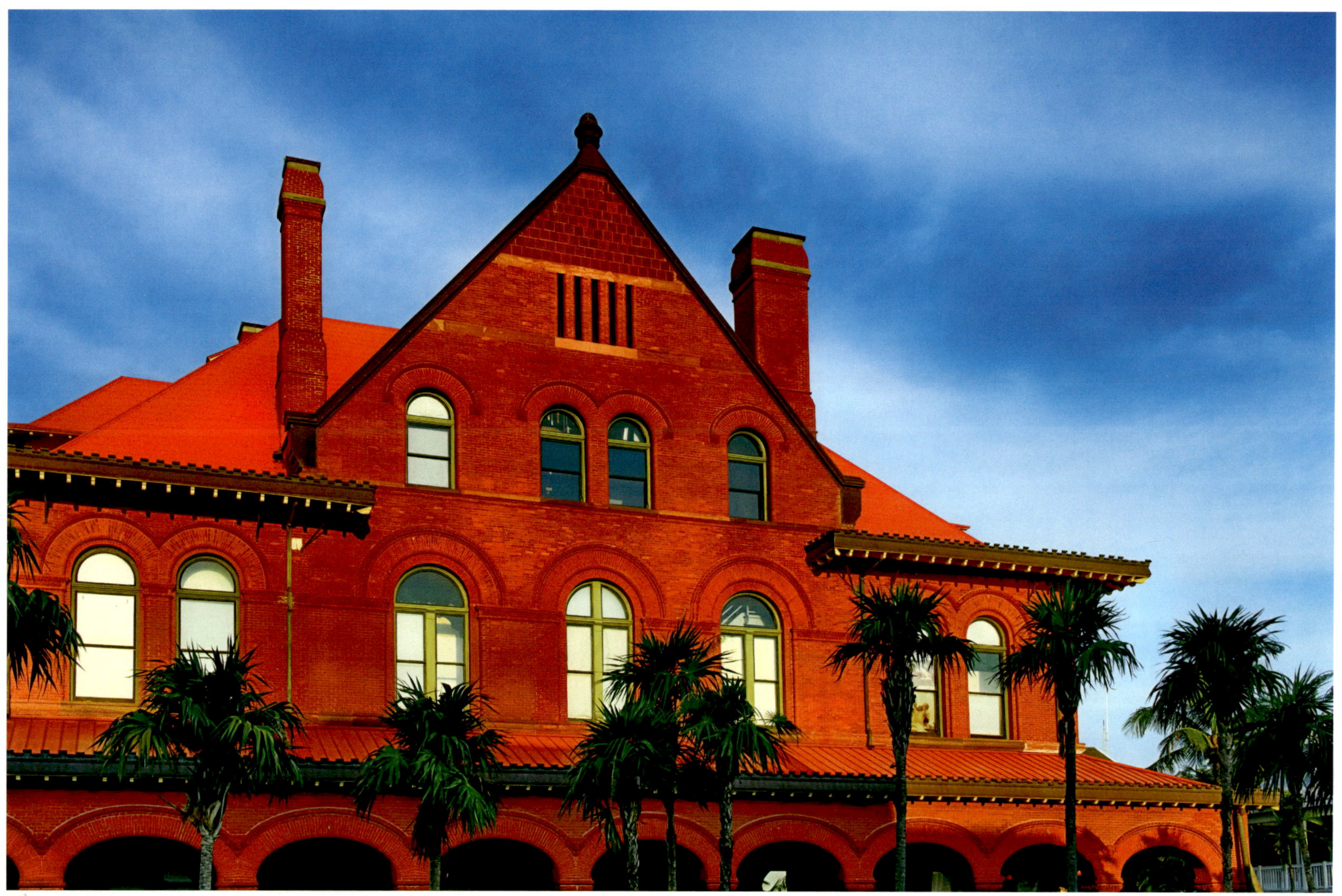

Customs House: Built in 1891 this building was once a post office, customs house, and Federal courthouse where shipwreck salvage cases were heard. The inquiry into the sinking of the USS Maine was held here. It is Romanesque Revival architecture, the finest in the state, constructed of red brick with stone and terra-cotta trim.

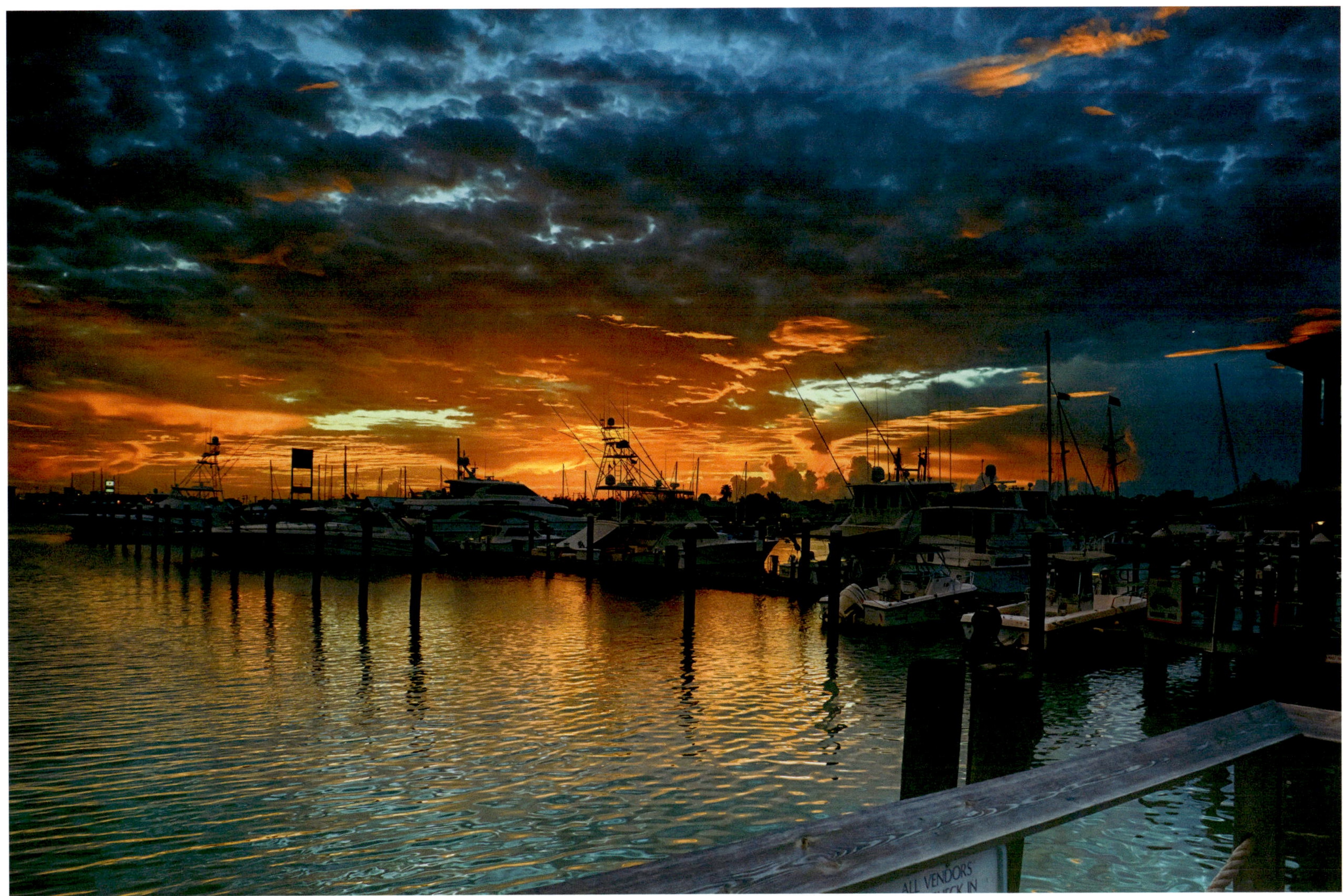

Key West Bight Sunrise: I usually scout out the location of each shot days ahead of time. This particular morning I was shooting the building at Front and Duval streets, as planned. When I was finished I looked east and said, “Holy Mackerel!” I ran down Front Street as fast as I could. I took a left at the end of the street, set up my tripod and this was my very first shot. In Key West, you never know what may happen!

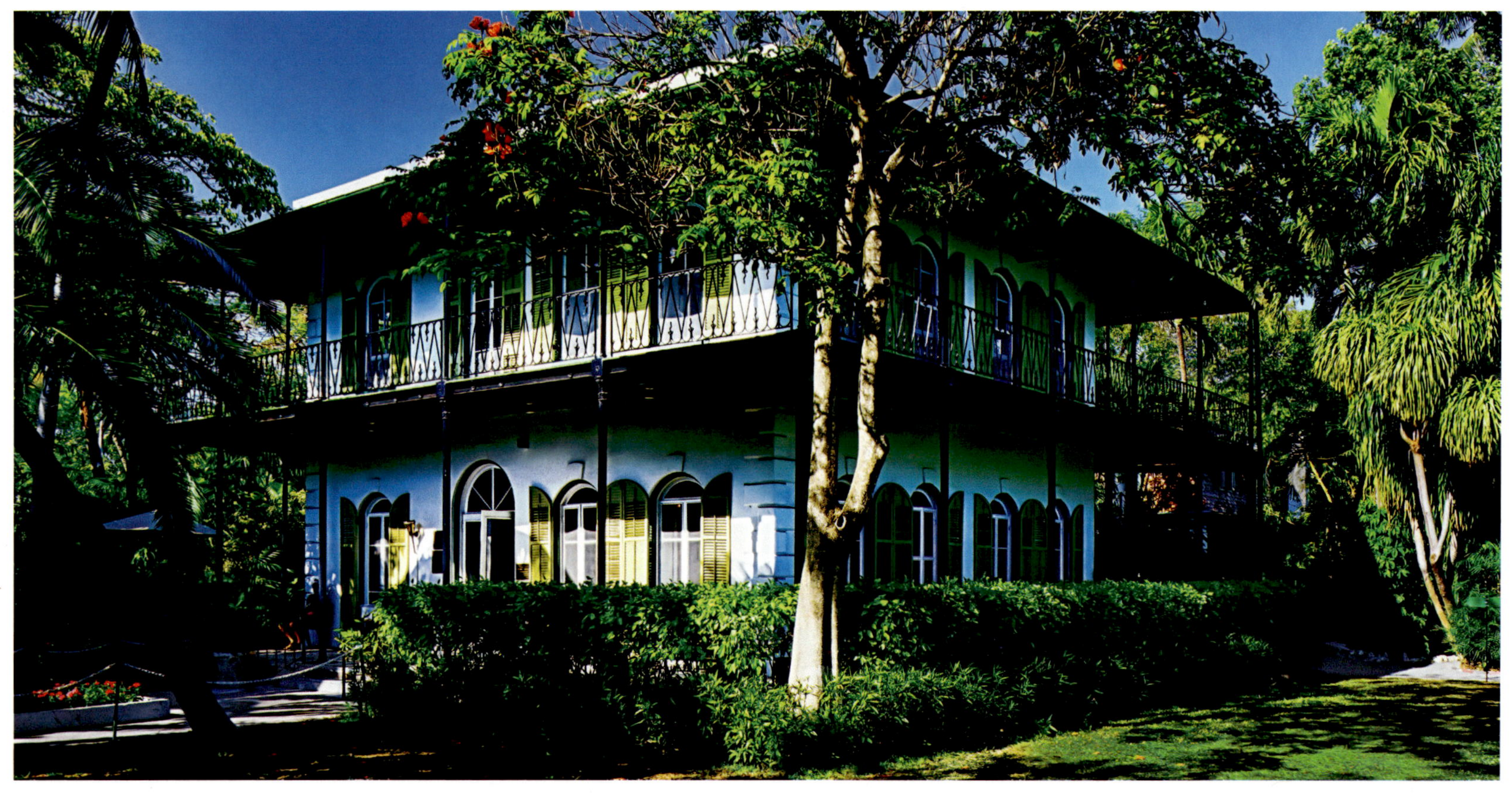

Hemingway's Home: This house was built in the 1850s by Asa Tift in the French Colonial style, the only one in Key West. Ernest and Pauline Hemingway lived here for nearly ten years, starting in 1931. This is where Hemingway did some of his best work including: *To Have or Have Not, For Whom the Bell Tolls,* and *A Farewell to Arms*.

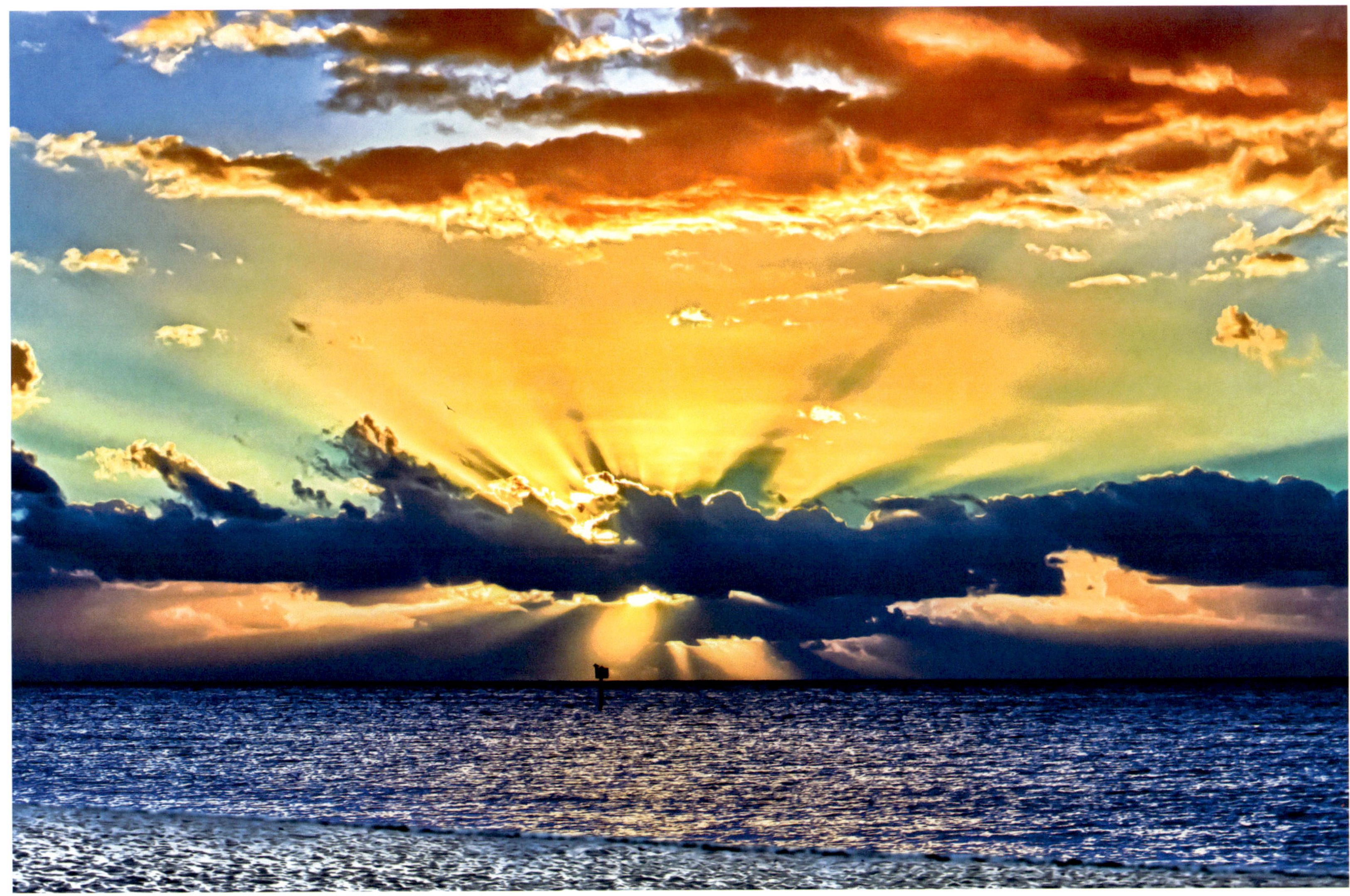

Sun Rays Sunrise: Sunrise at Smathers Beach in Key West on November 26, 2011. A truly spectacular sunrise.

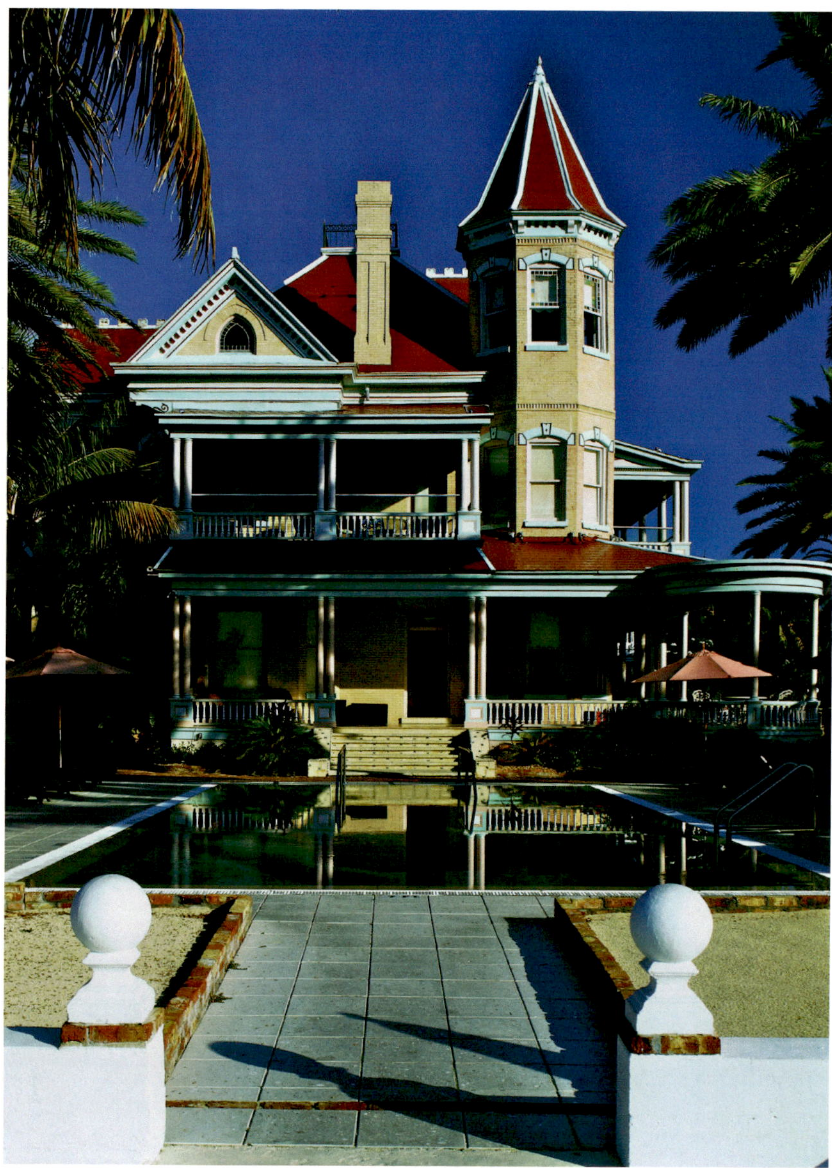

Southernmost House Pool: The Southern Most House, also known as the Judge Vining Harris home was built in 1896. It is Victorian Queen Anne architecture.

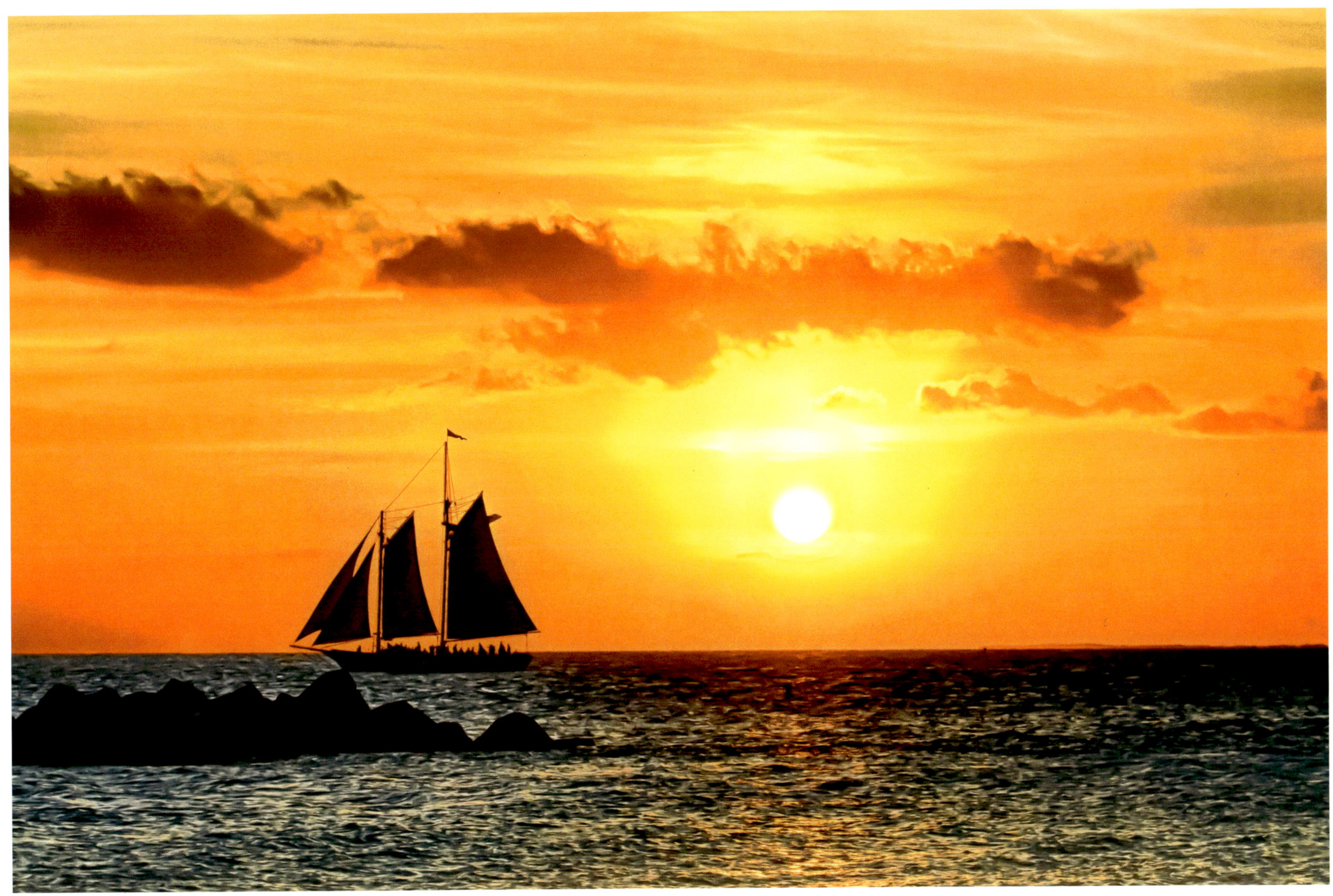

Layers Sunset Schooner: Sunset in Key West on February 21, 2012. As you can see, the clouds form layers of different shades and hues.

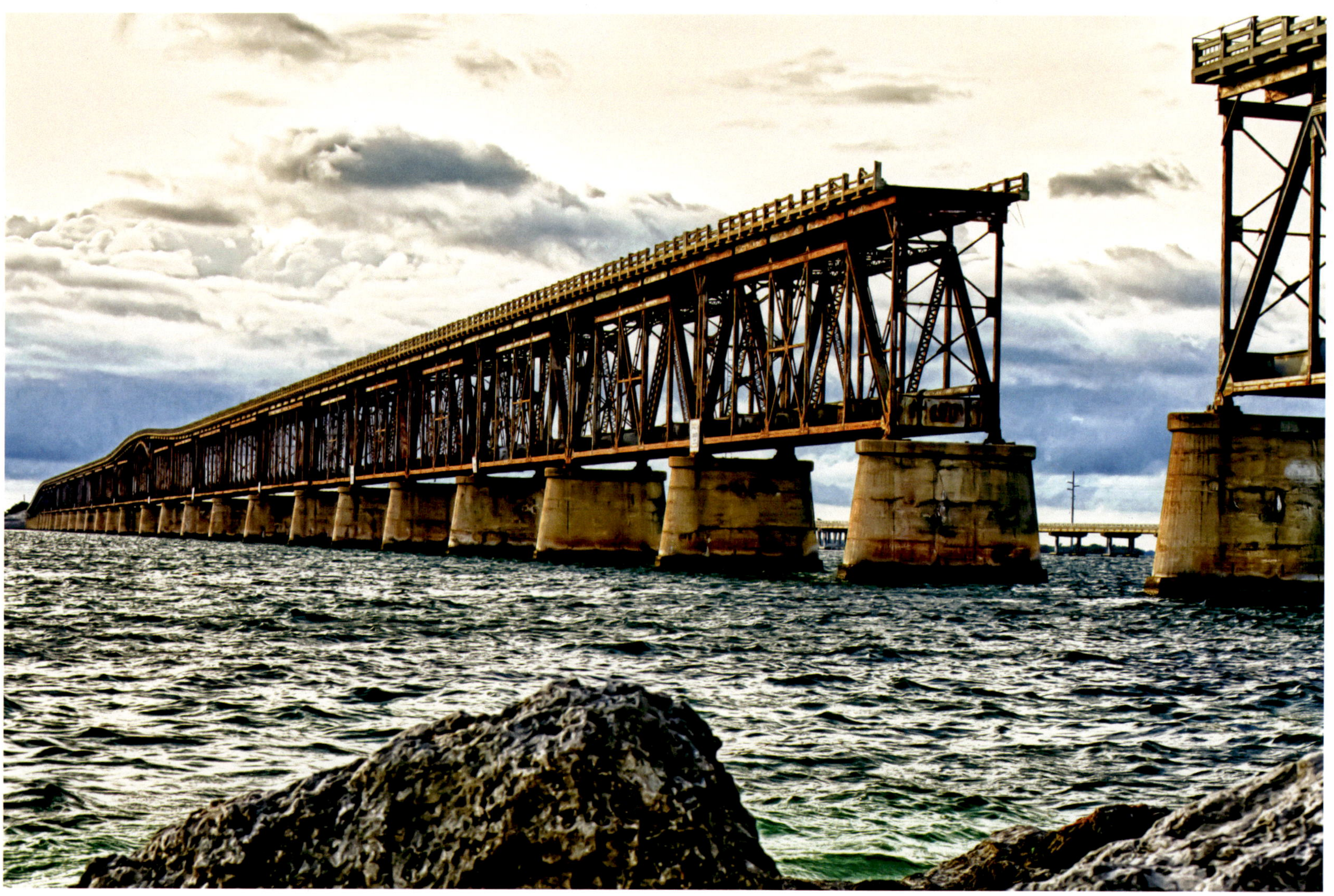

Bahia Honda Bridge: Shot at Bahia Honda State Park, Florida on January 2, 2012. This was the last bridge that was completed during the construction of the Overseas Railroad. When they finished it in early January 1912, Key West was connected to the mainland for the first time. A few days later, on January 22, 1912, Henry Flagler rode the very first train into Key West!

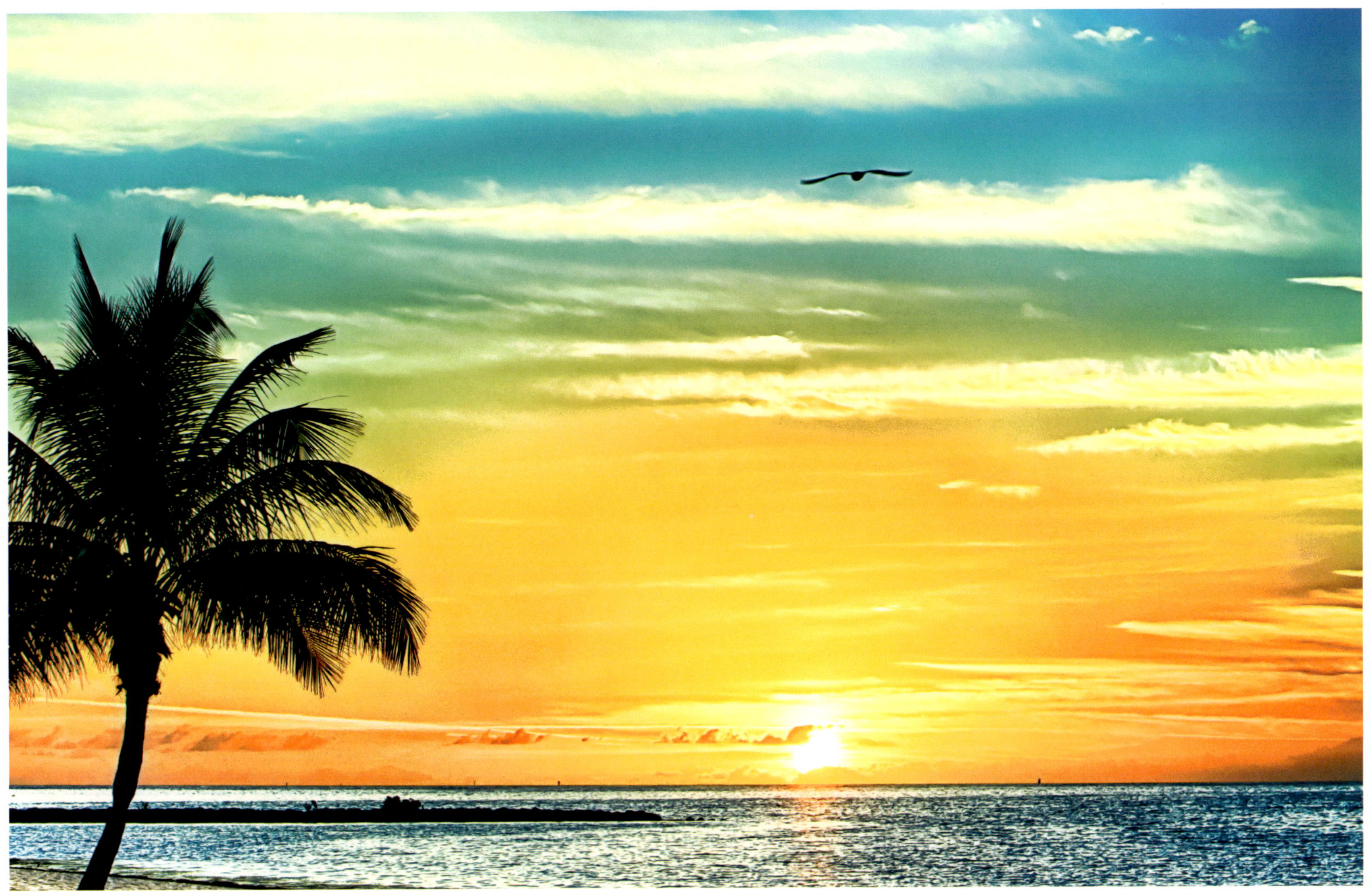

Sunrise Burst: A seagull rises with the sun in Key West. This was shot the same morning as "Key West Magical Sunrise." What a day!

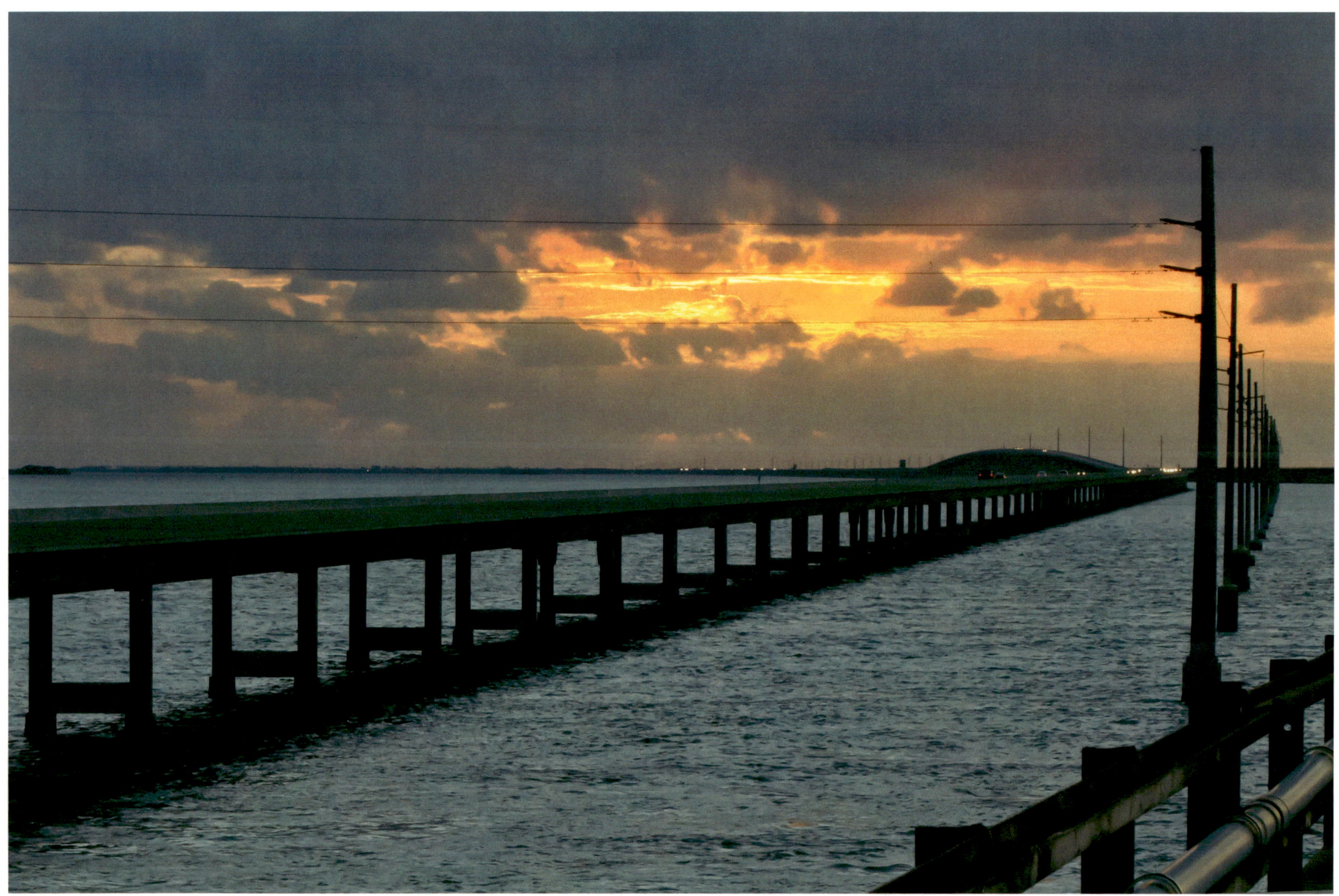

Seven Mile Bridge Sunset: Sunset at the Seven Mile Bridge on February 13, 2012.

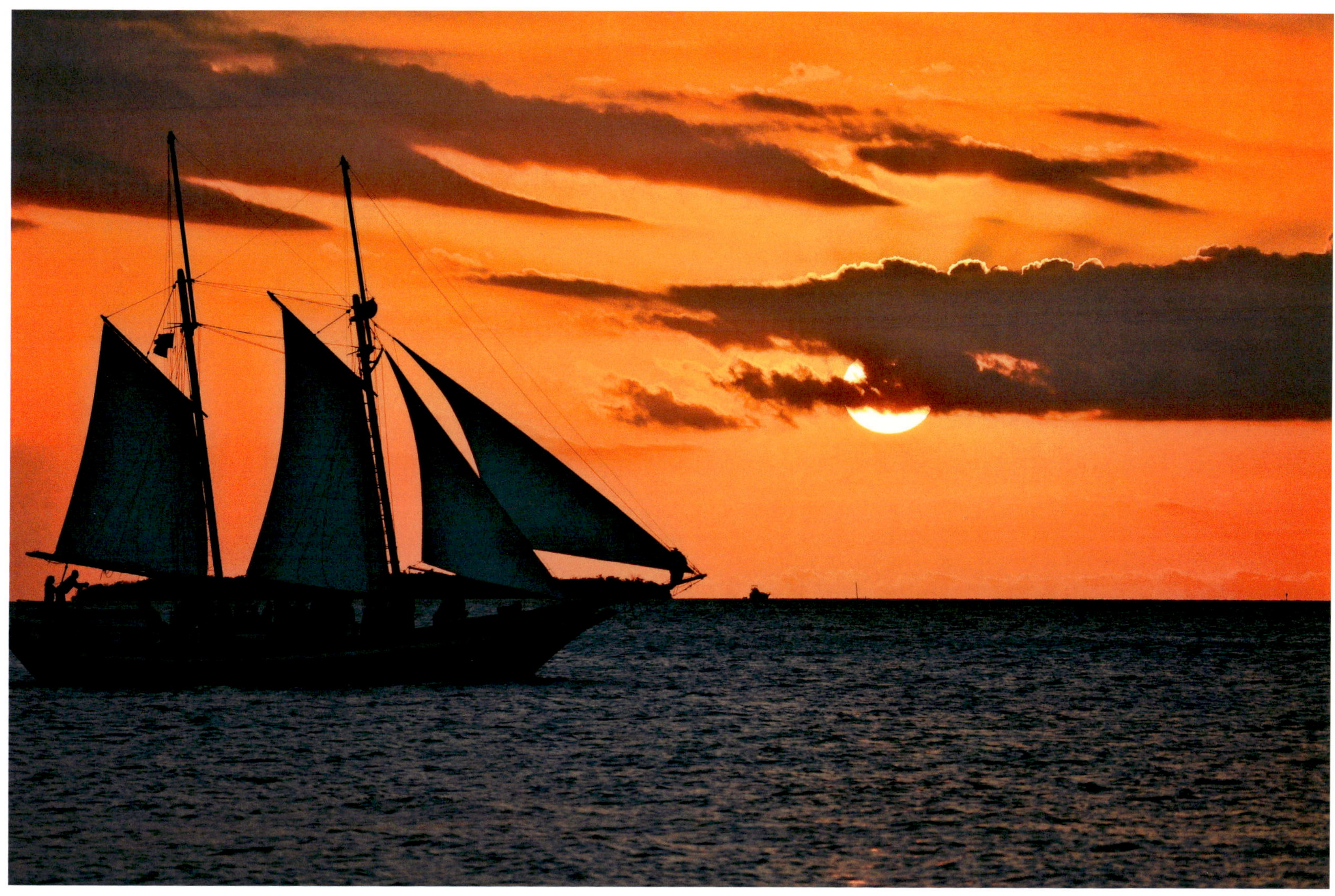

Cloud Sails: Clouds mirror the schooner's sails on May 22, 2010.

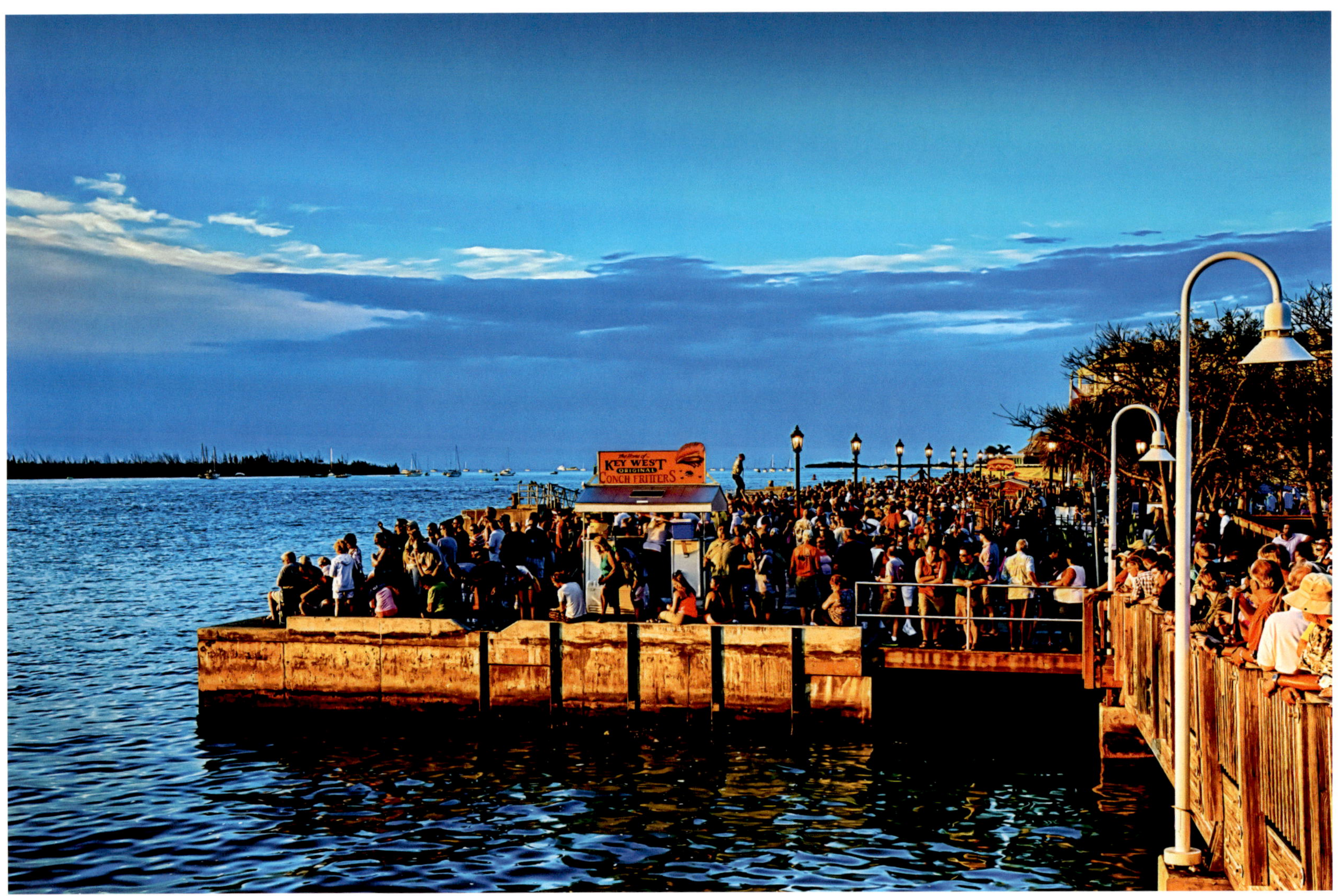

Mallory Square Sunset Celebration: The famous daily ritual in Key West.

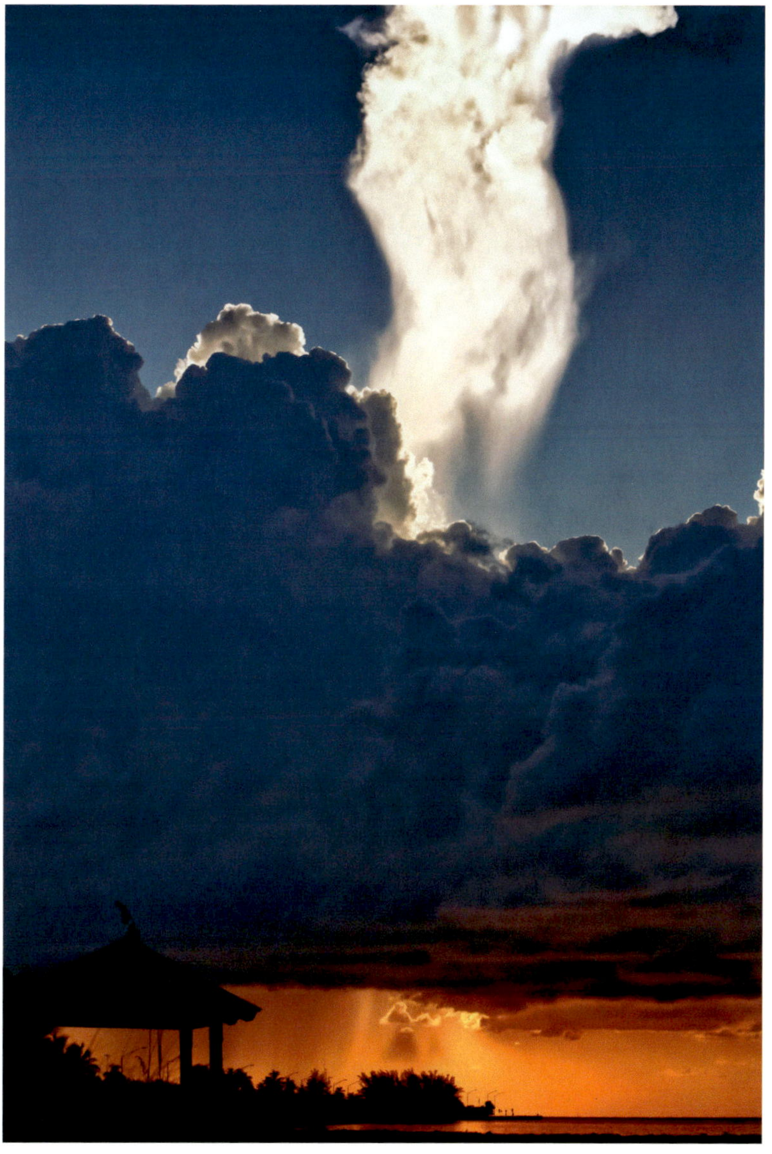

Vertical Cloud Sunrise: A thunderhead cloud provides a dramatic sunrise. An incredible and unique view on the morning of September 15, 2011.

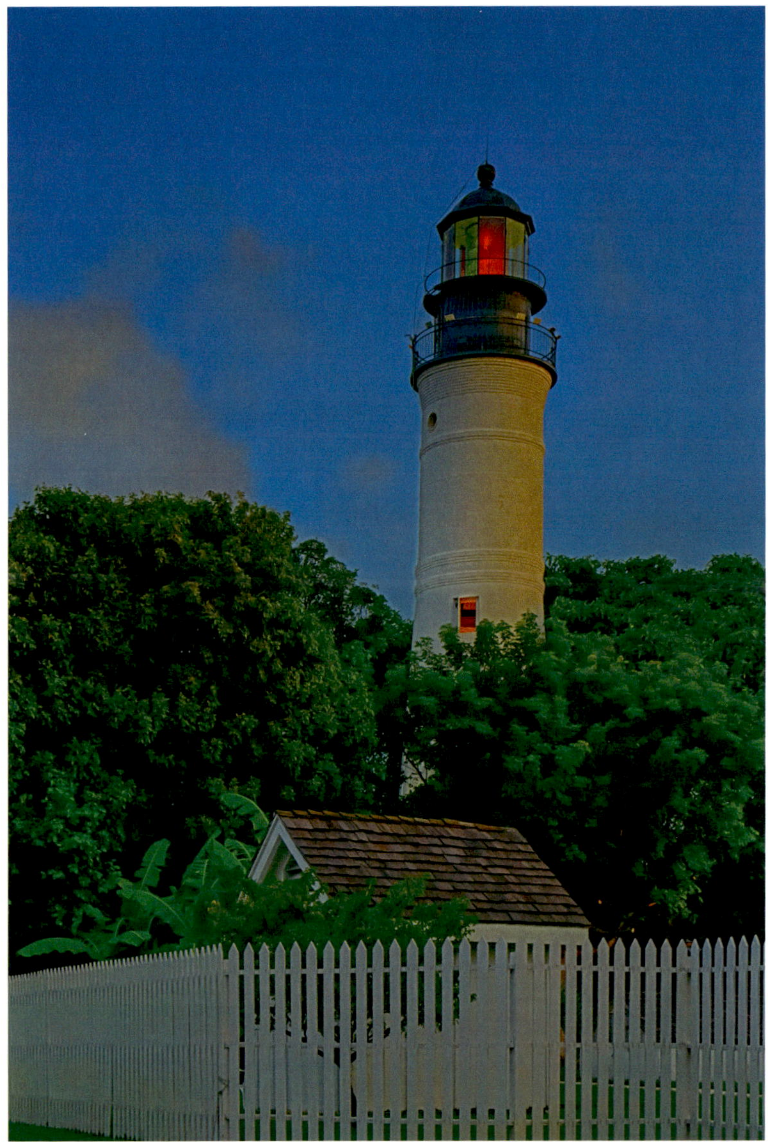

Key West Lighthouse: The original lighthouse was built in 1825 down by the Southernmost Point, but was destroyed in the terrible hurricane of 1846. This one was built in 1847.

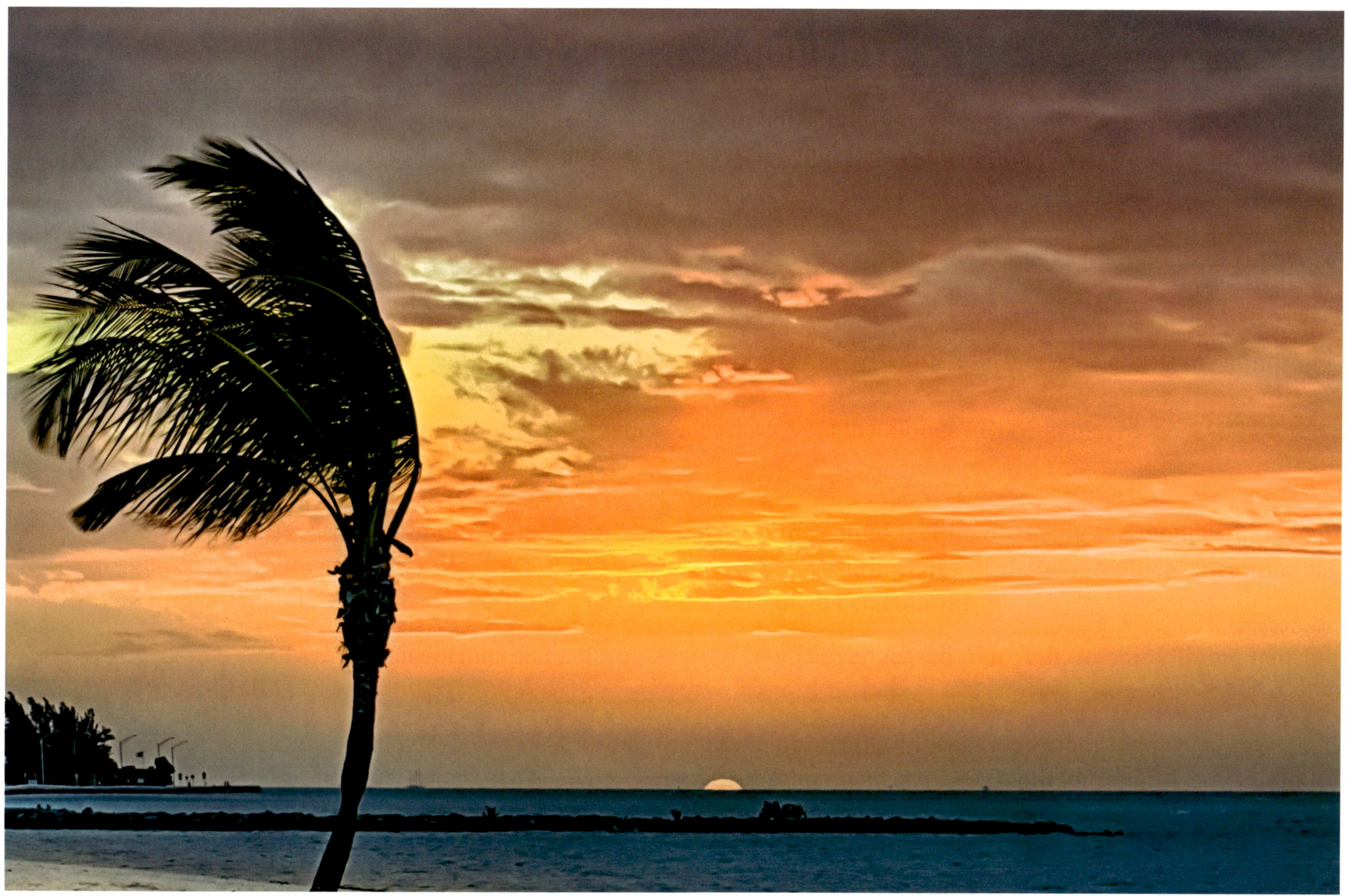

Windy Sunrise: It was so windy it took some time to clean all the sand off my Nikon D800 when I got home, but it was well worth it. The different layers of clouds are inspiring.

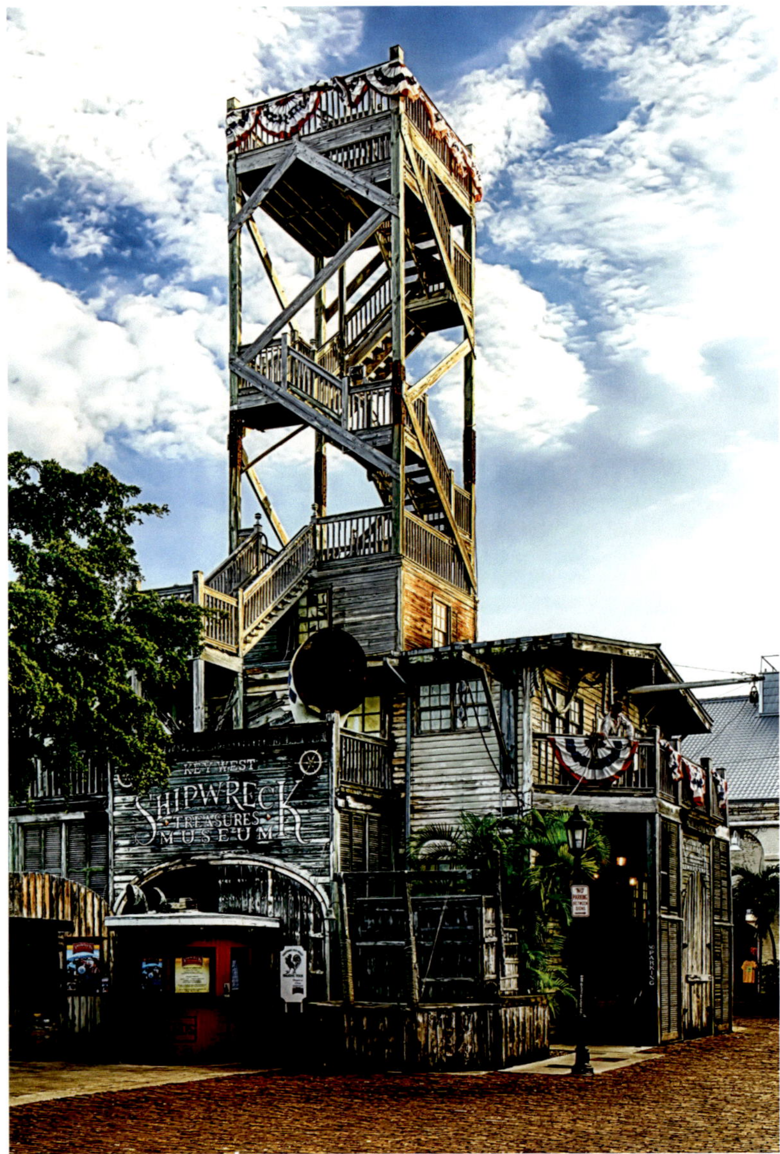

Shipwreck Treasure Museum: Key West's Shipwreck Treasure Museum in Mallory Square. Climb the tower for a great view of the island!

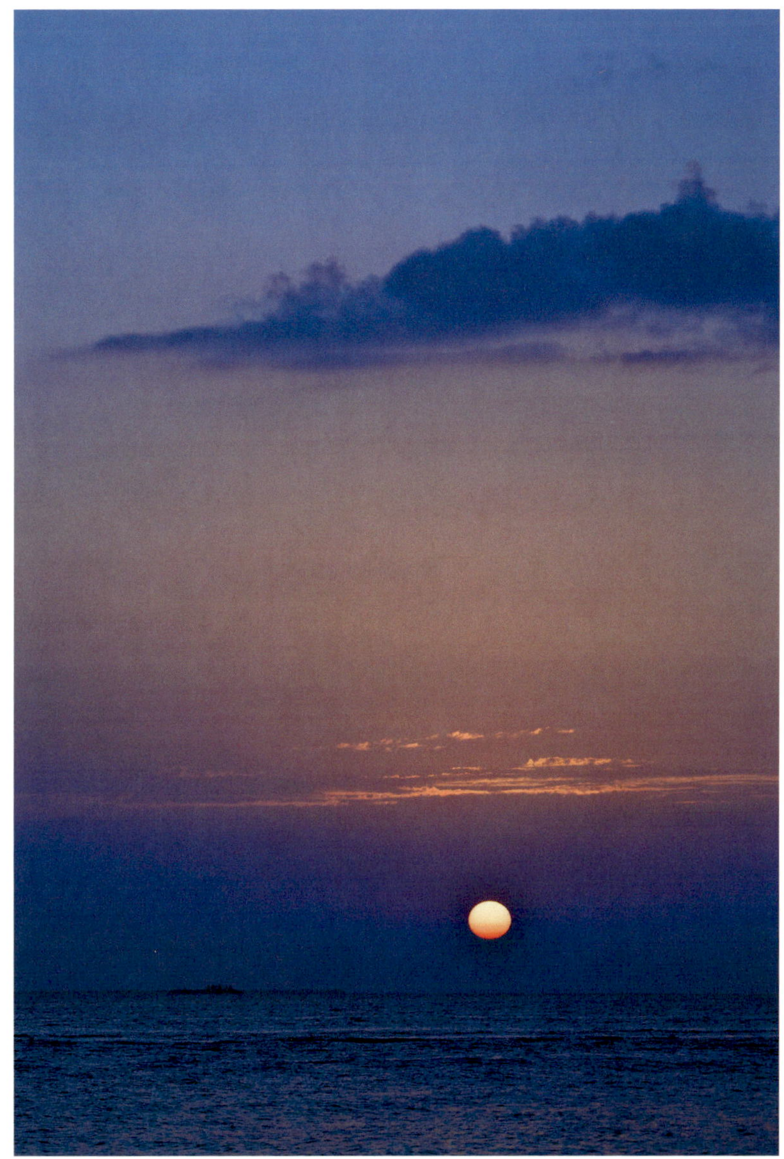

Blue Cloud: A truly serene, blue sunset in Key West.

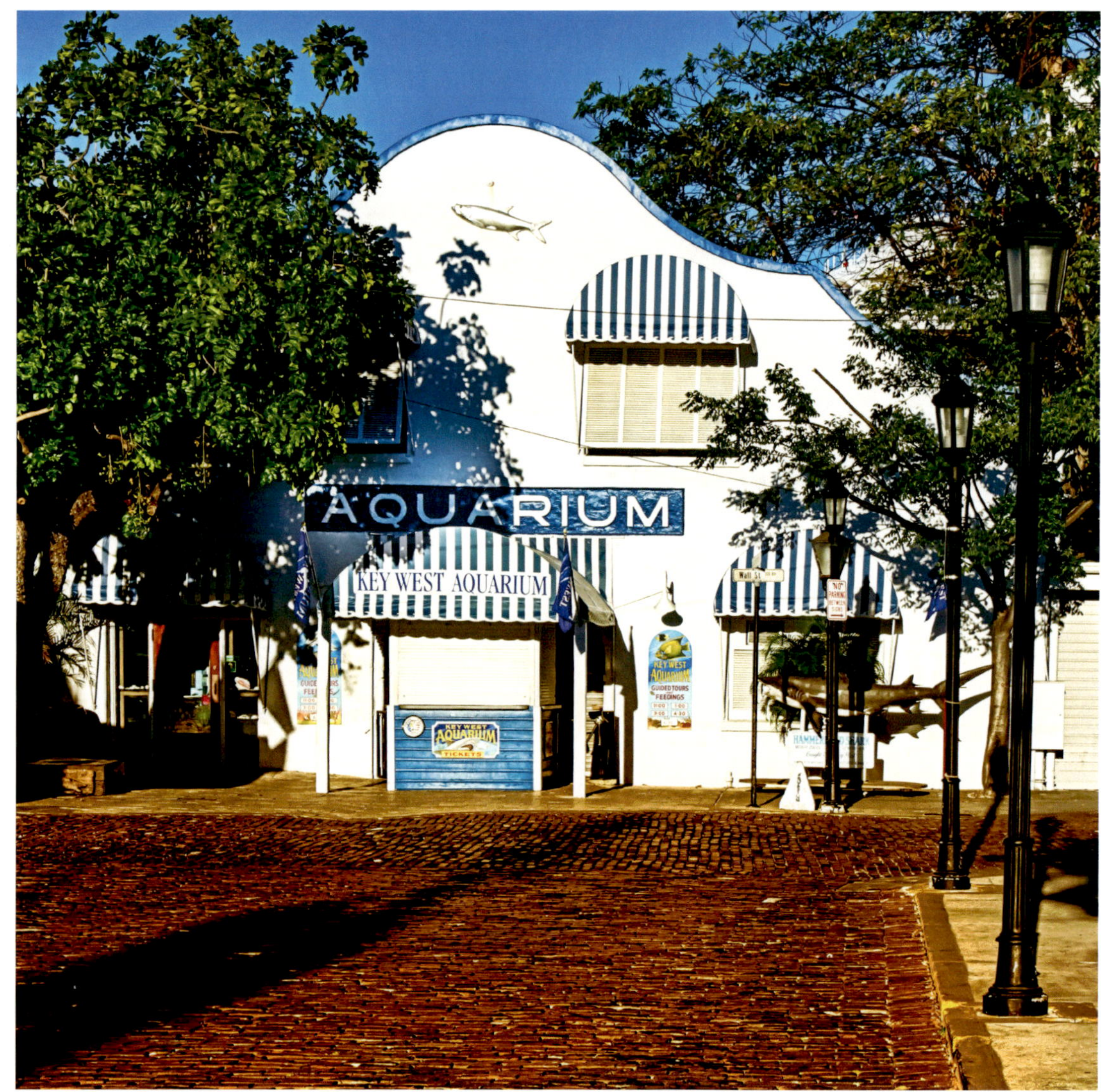

Key West Aquarium: Built in 1934, this was Key West's first tourist attraction. Go to the aquarium and pet a live shark!

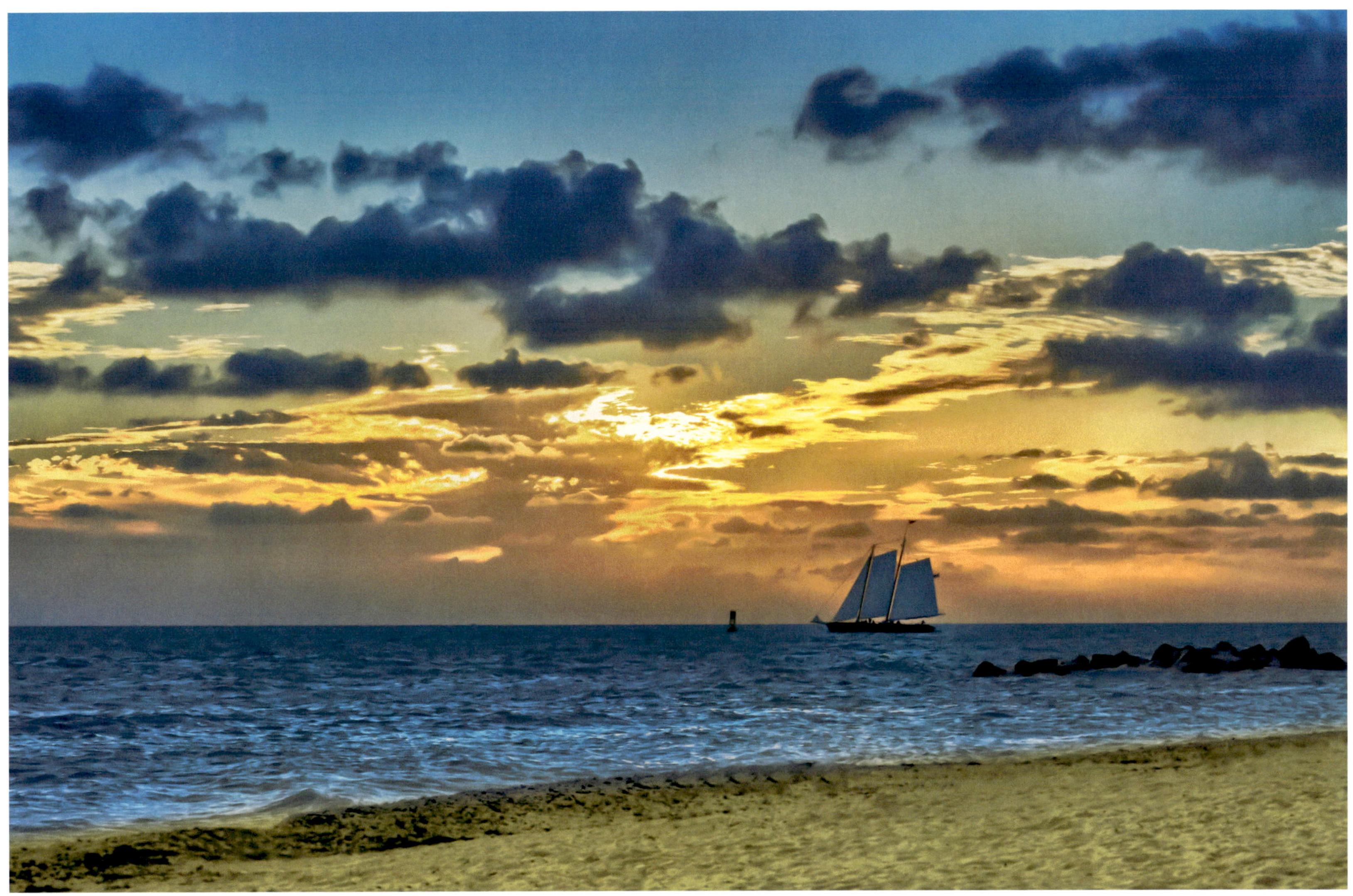

Brilliant Schooner Sunset: A Schooner passes Ft. Zachary Taylor State Park on December 20, 2011.

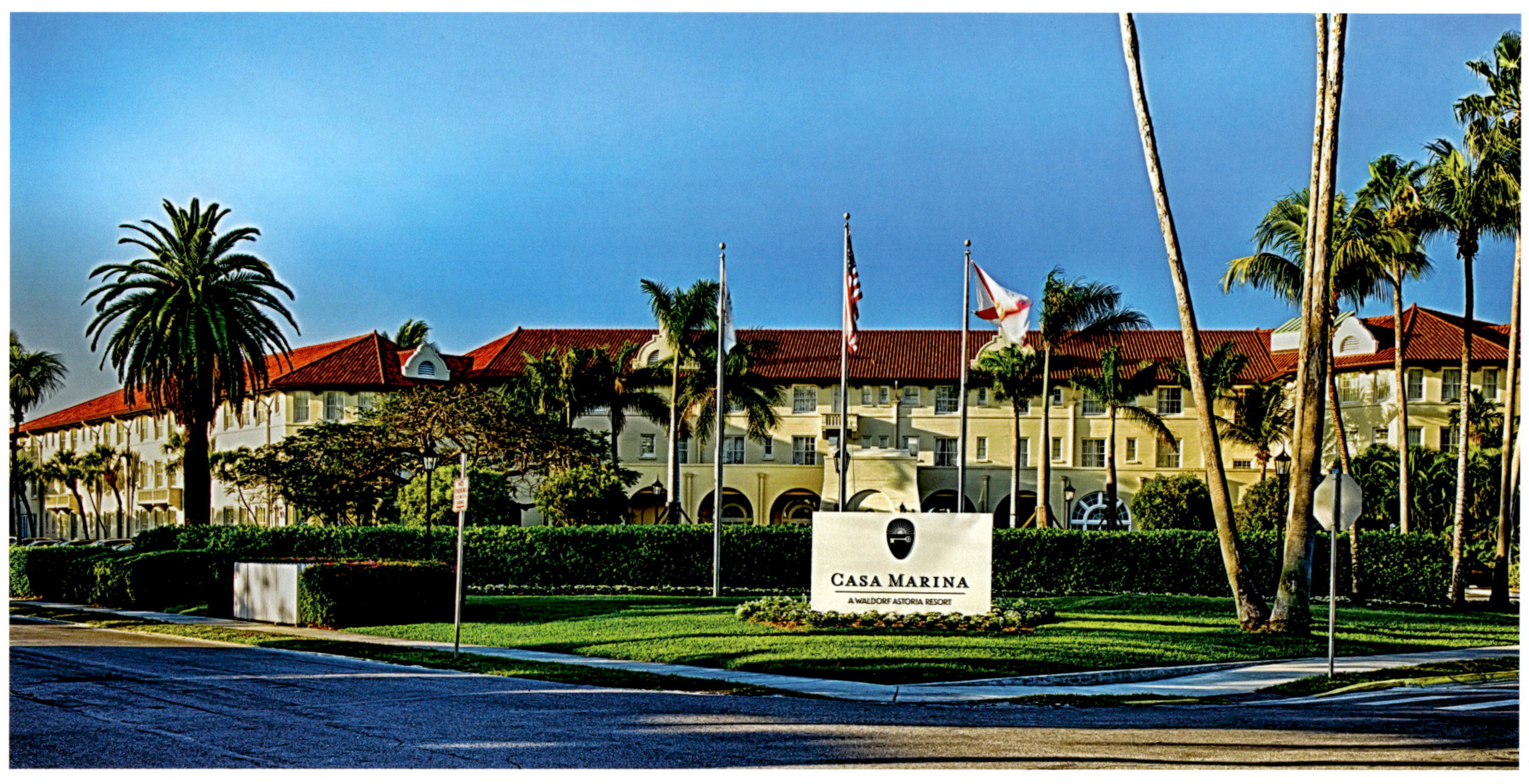

Casa Marina: Henry Flagler built a luxury hotel for his passengers at each stop along his railroad. Construction of the Casa Marina started in 1918 and the hotel opened New Years Eve 1920.

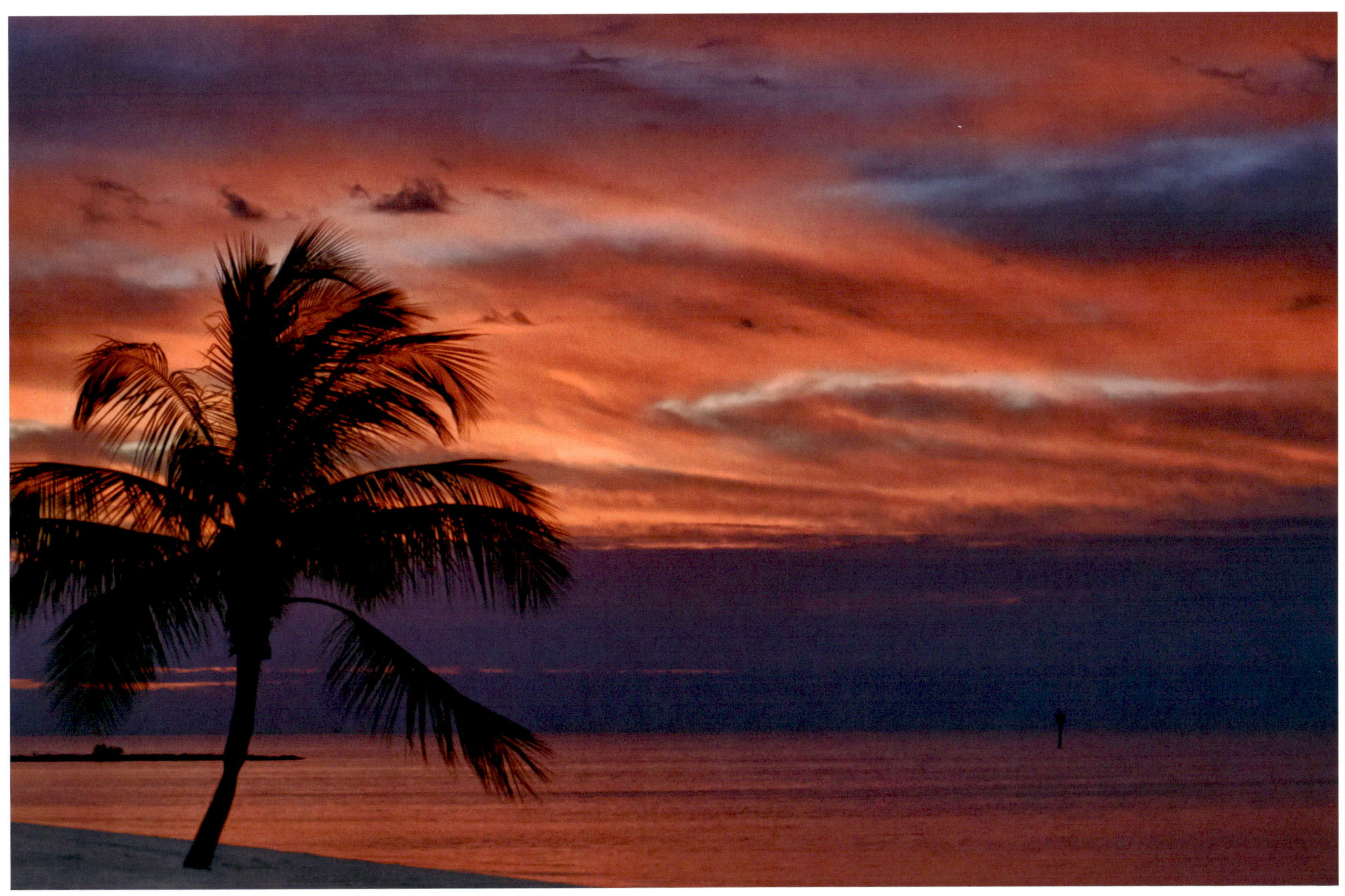

Morning Twilight Magic: Twilight colors at Smathers Beach on October 24, 2011. A truly magical morning. I've heard that twilight colors like this happen all the time in Hawaii, but this is rare in Key West.

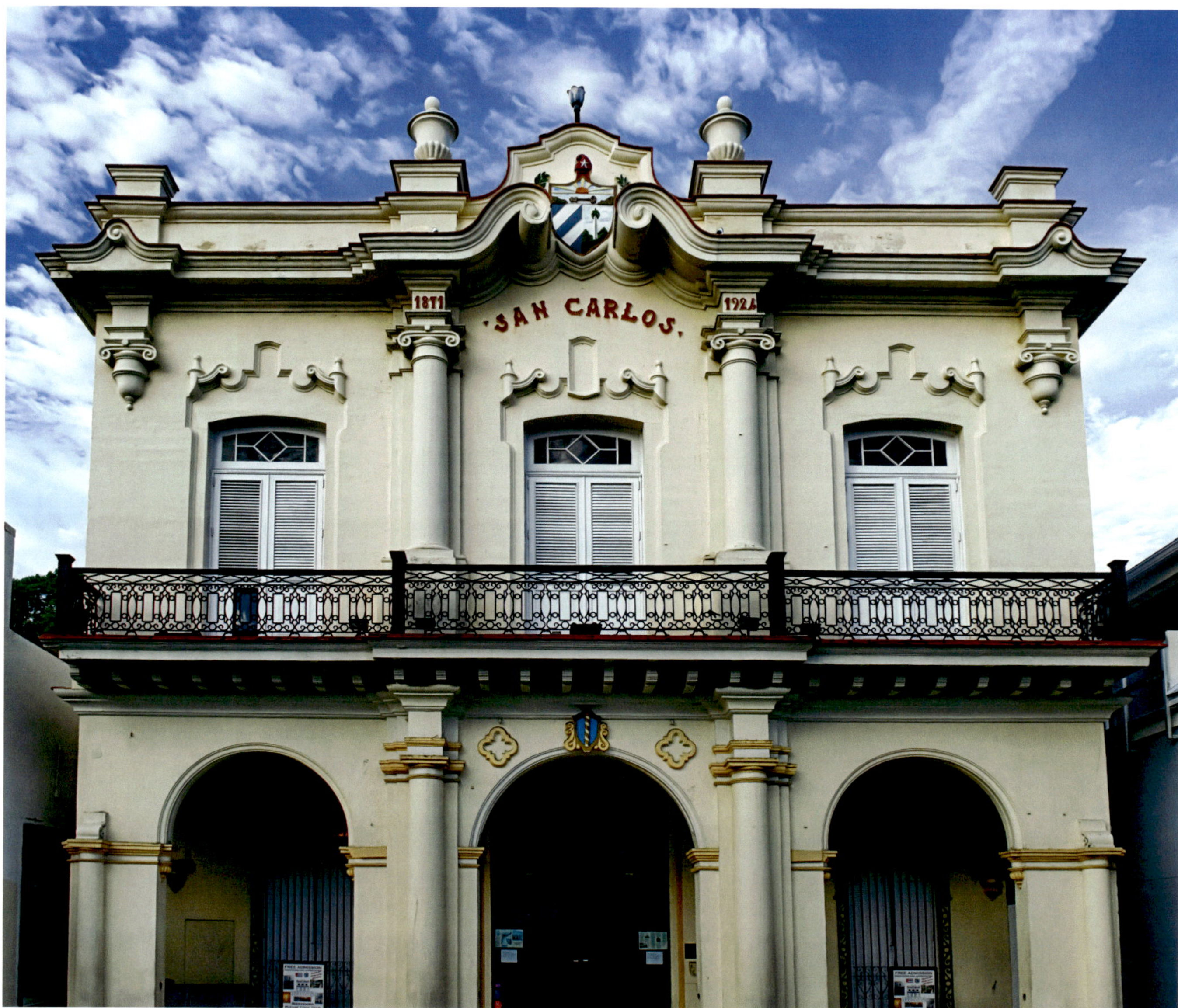

San Carlos Institute: In 1871 a group of Cuban patriots formed the San Carlos Institute as a place to conspire for Cuba's independence from Spain. This structure was built in 1924 and is modeled after Havana City Hall. Today it's a cultural center and a museum.

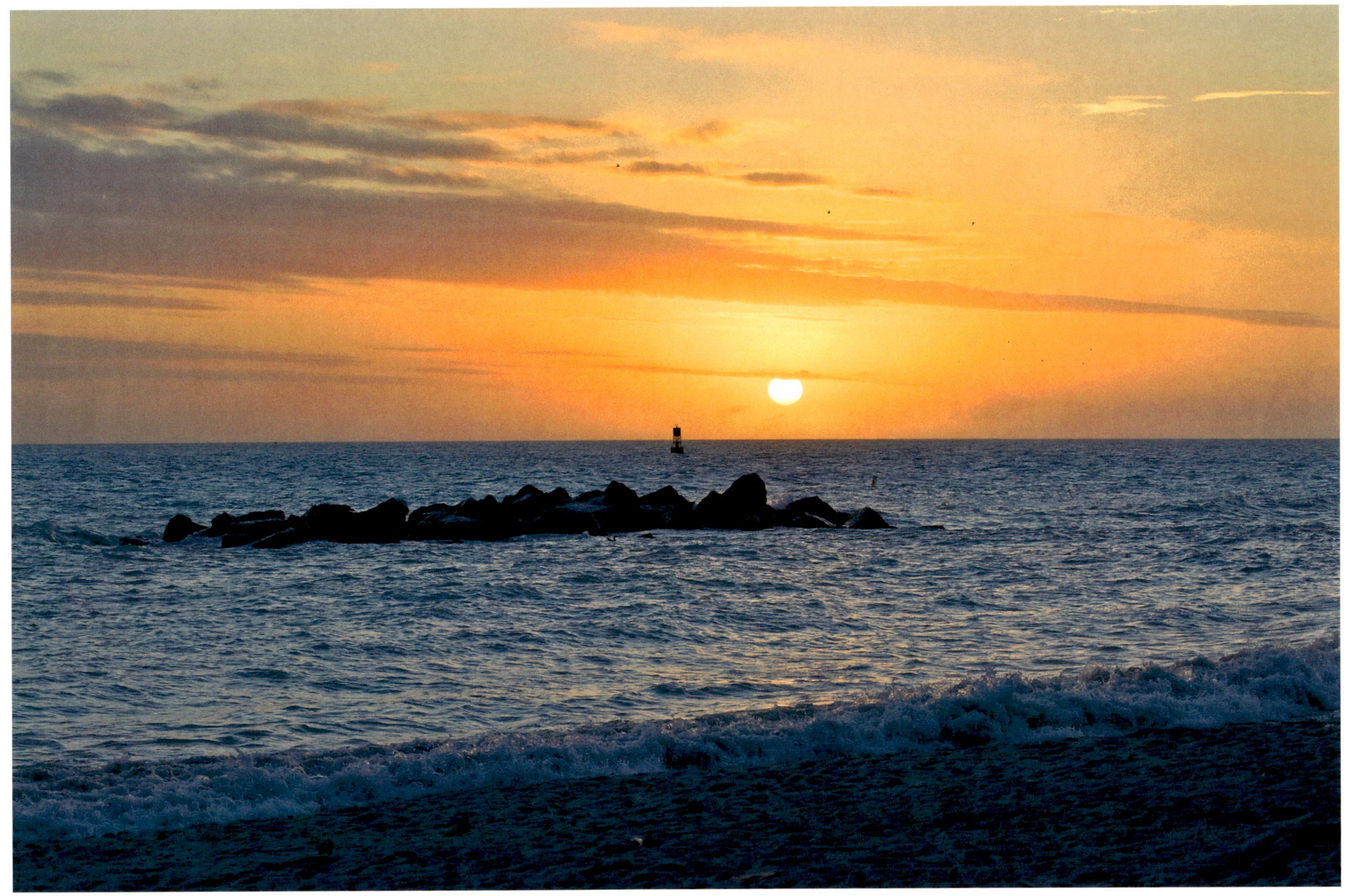

Beach Rocks: A gorgeous sunset for the last day of 2010.

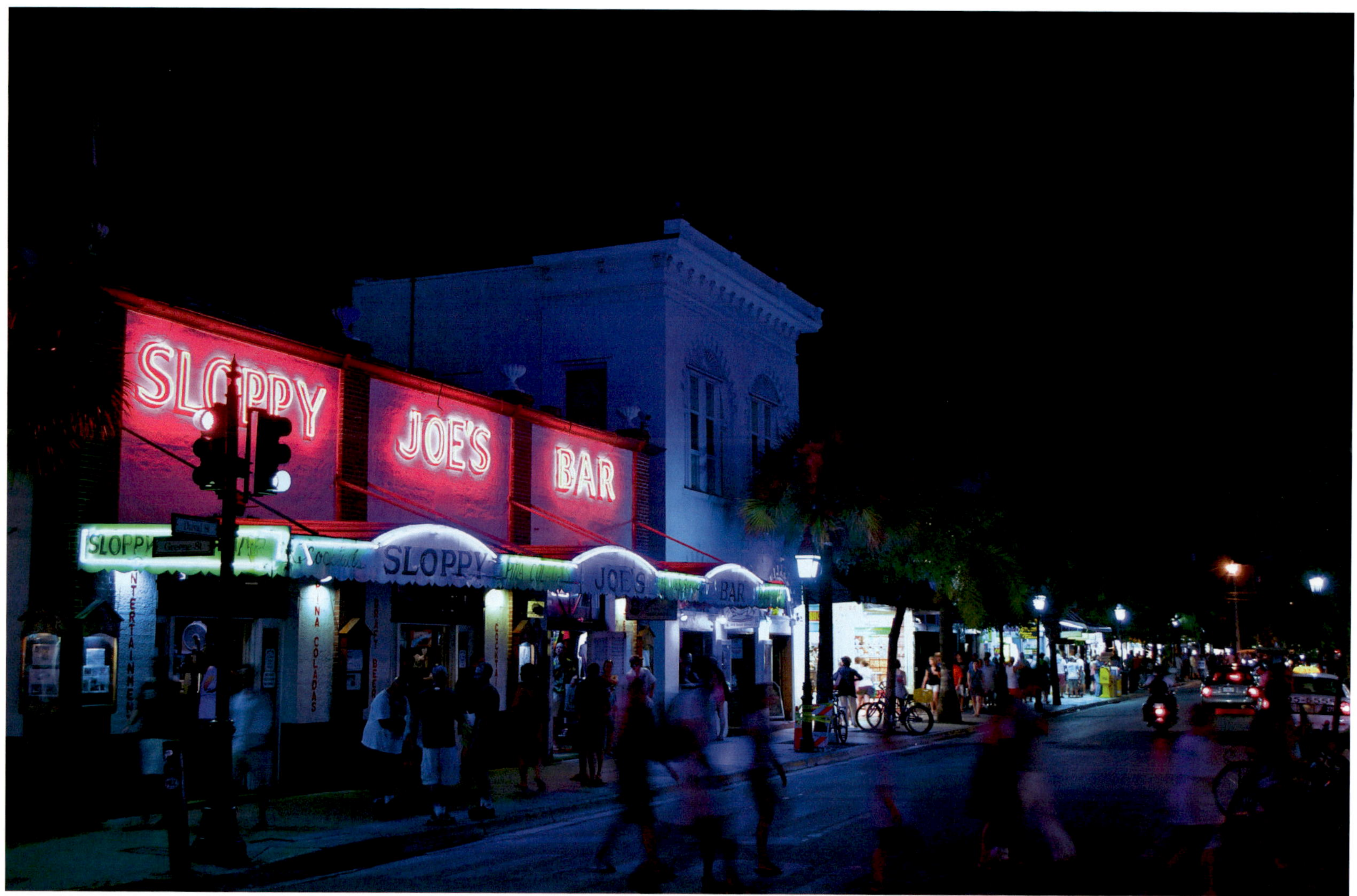

Sloppy Joe's: The most famous bar in Key West, Sloppy Joe's was Ernest Hemingway's favorite bar. It was built by his fishing buddy Sloppy Joe Russell.

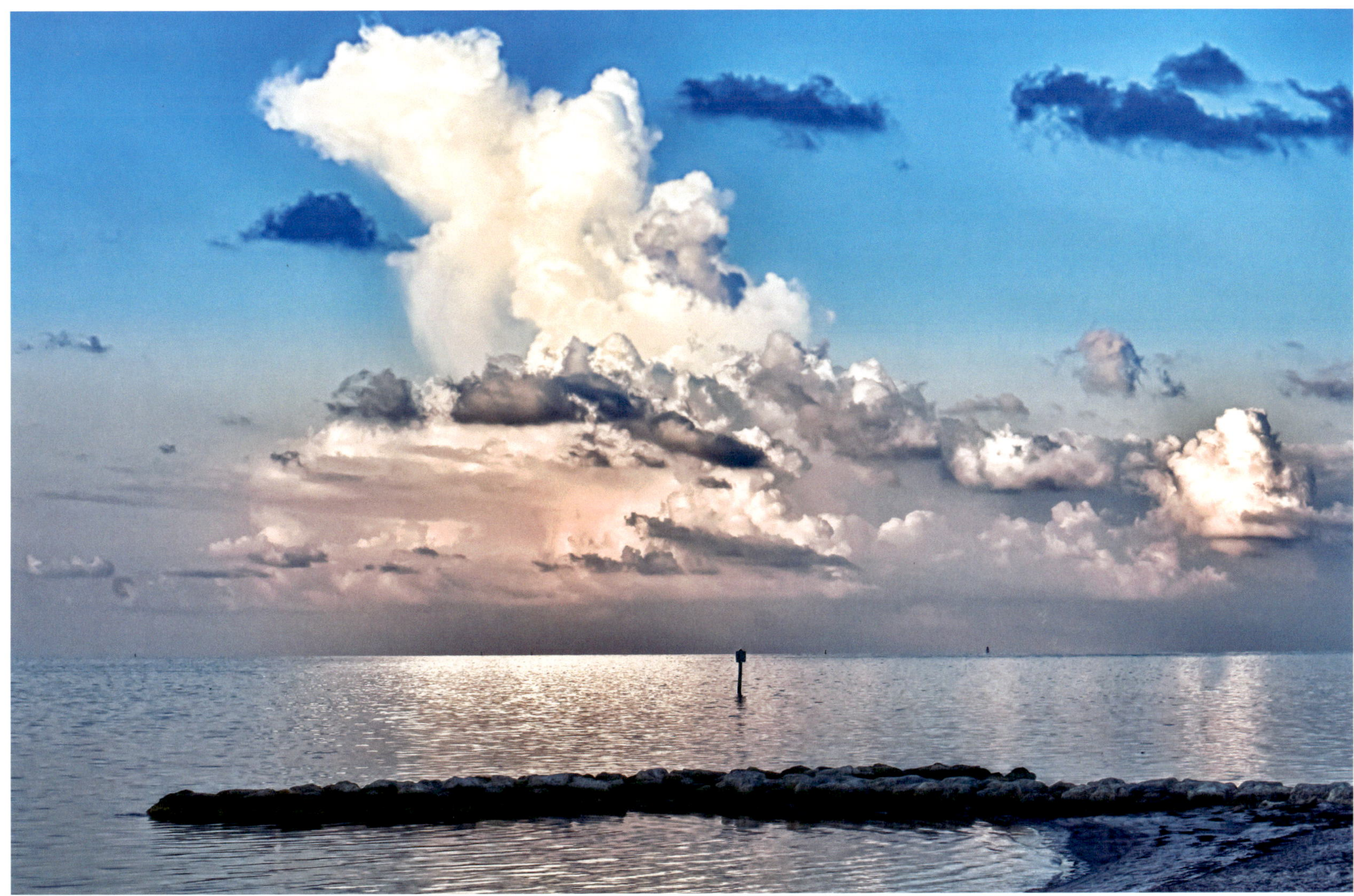

Cloudscape at Sunrise: The reflection on the metallic water and the variety of clouds make this shot three dimensional. This was shot on the same morning as "Vertical Cloud Sunrise."

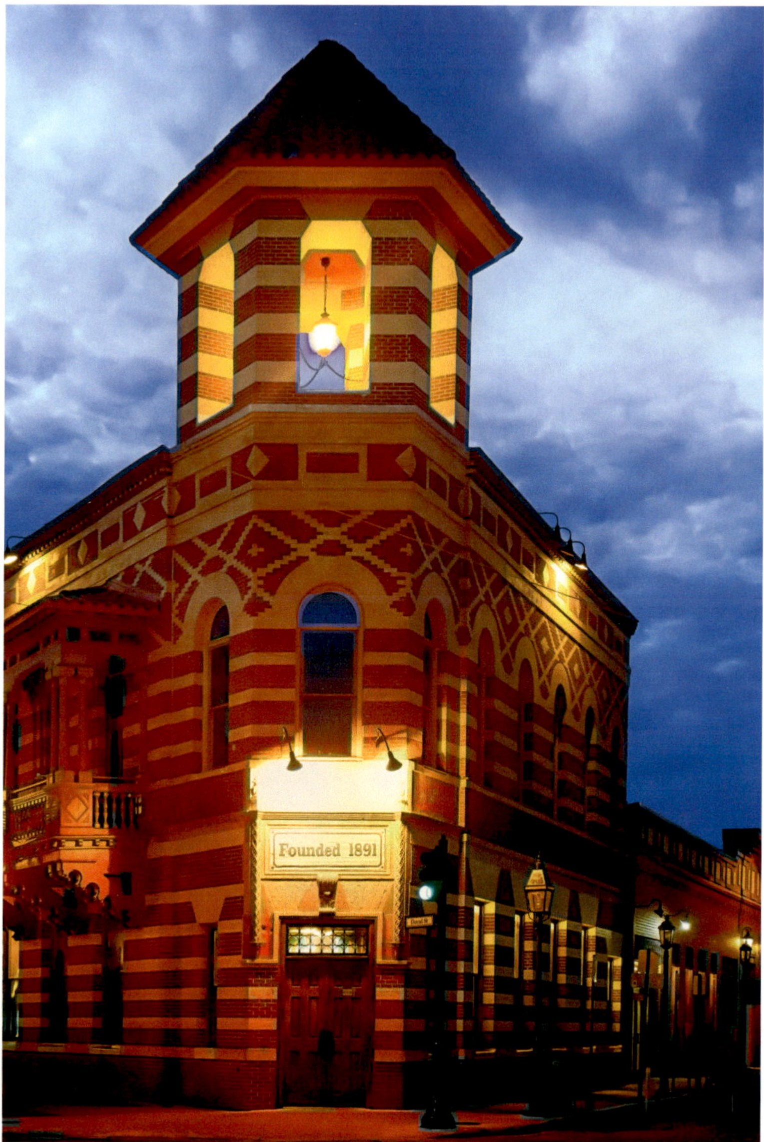

Duval and Front: This bank was first built in 1891 by Cuban cigar factory owners. It was featured as the bank that was robbed in Ernest Hemingway's novel *To Have and Have Not.*

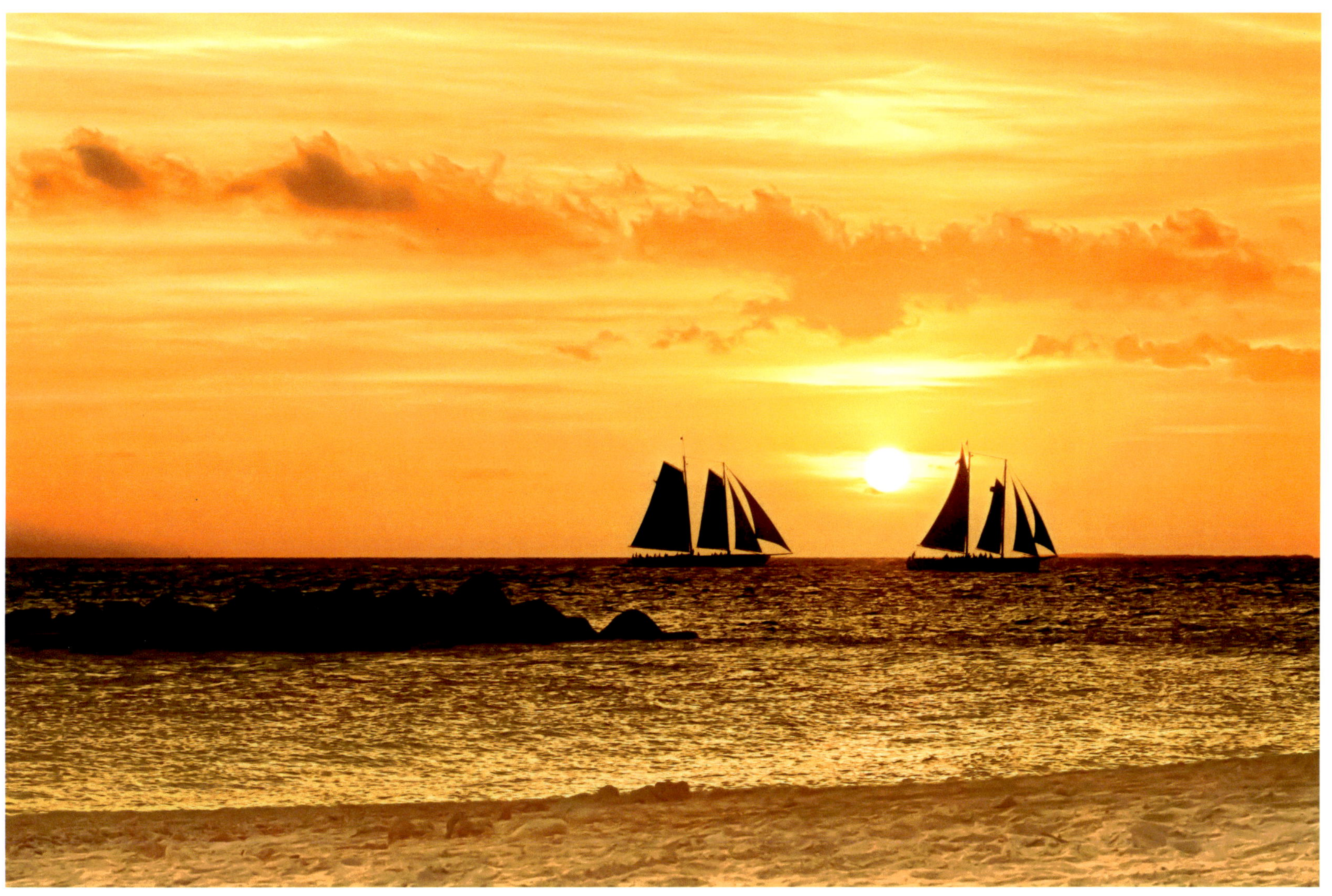

Pair of Schooners Sunset: Schooners cruise near shore as the sun makes the ocean sparkle!

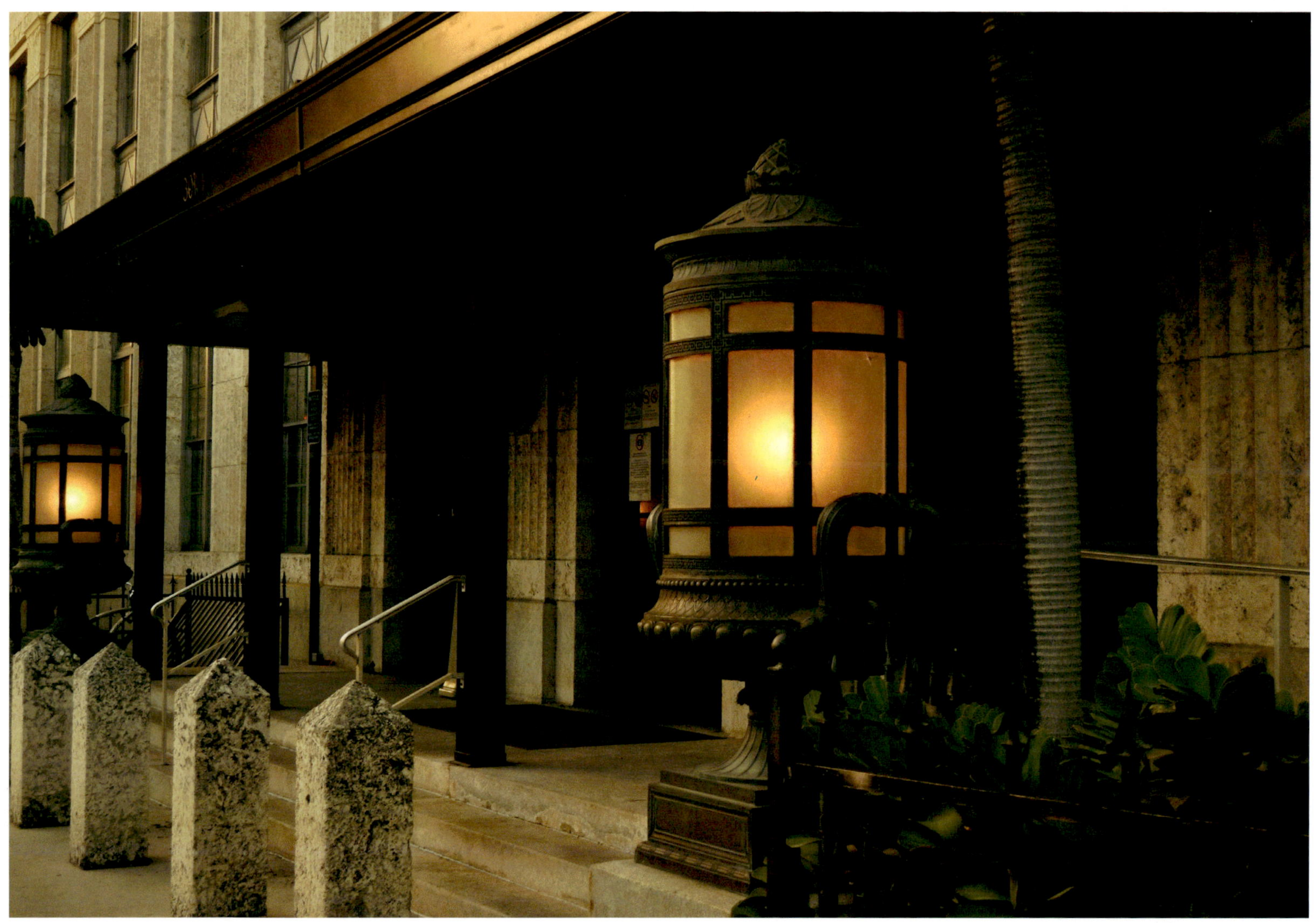

Chinese Lanterns: Chinese lanterns in front of the Federal Courthouse on Simonton Street. In the early 1900's a Chinese cargo ship made a stop in Key West and didn't have cash to pay the customs officer so they gave us these lanterns.

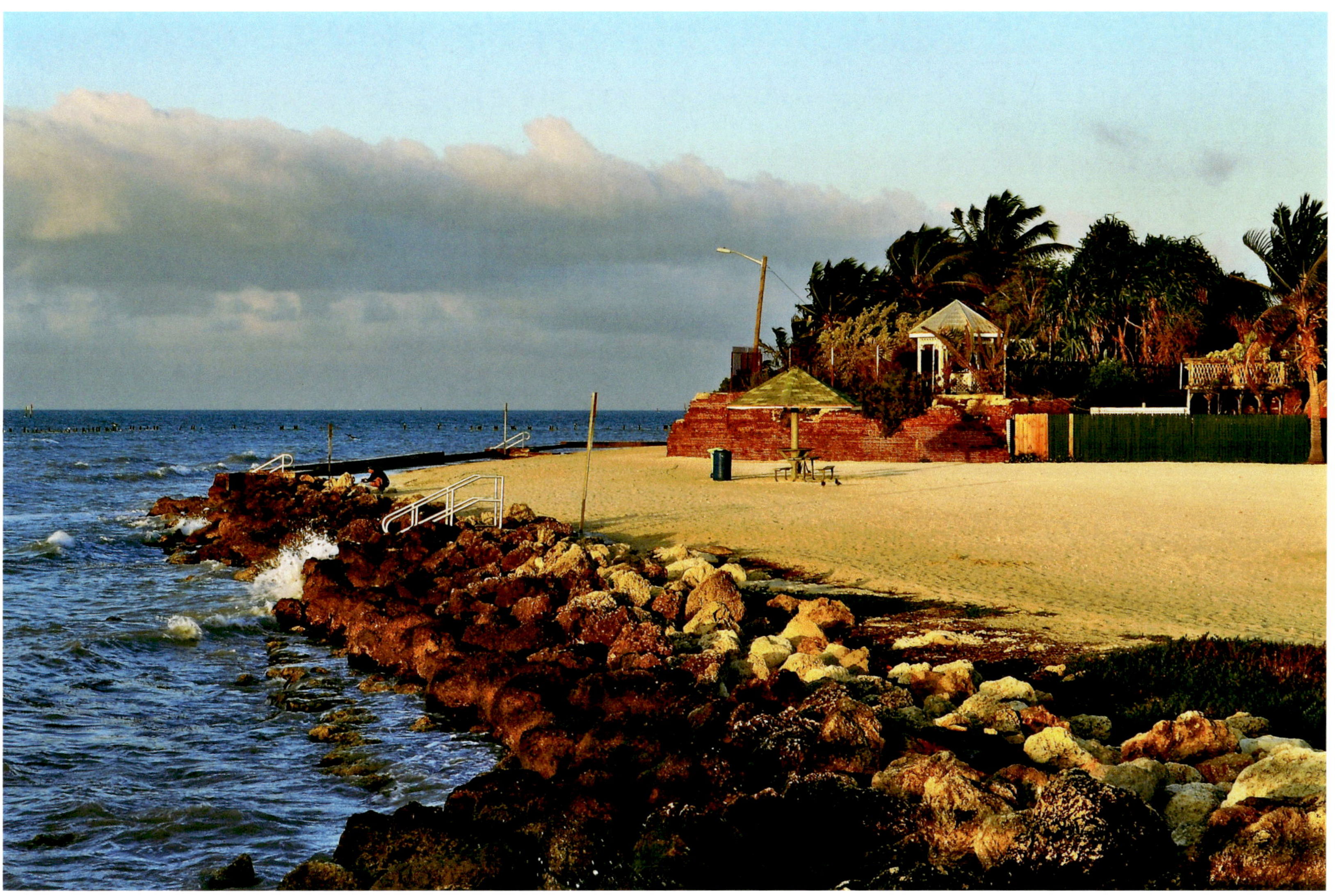

Higgs Beach: Shot on April 7, 2010 from the White Street pier in Key West.

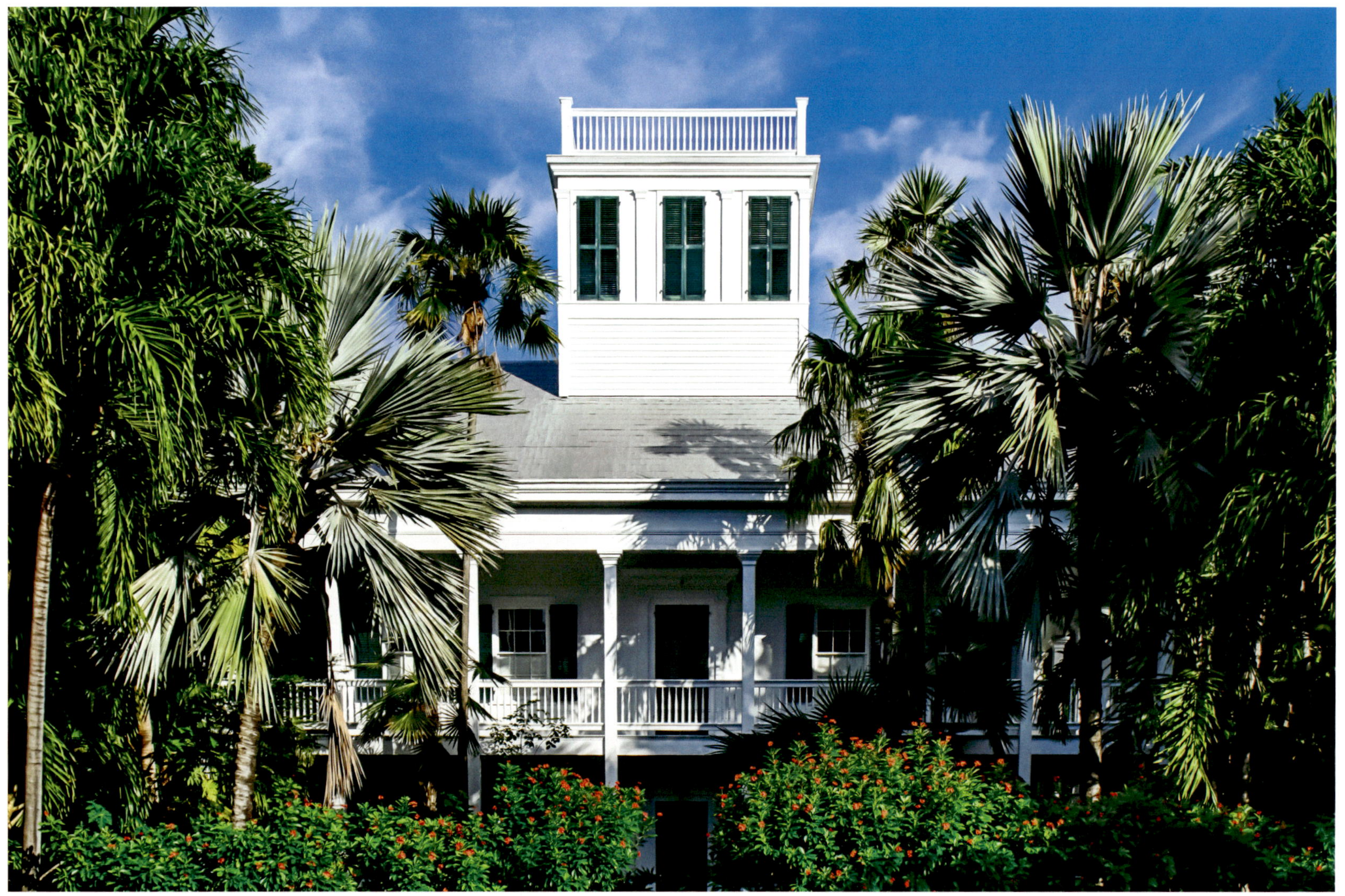

John Lowe Jr. House: The John Lowe Jr. home on Southard Street, with its famous Captain's Walk. Shipwreck captains stood on top, looking for shipwrecks on the coral reef, five miles offshore.

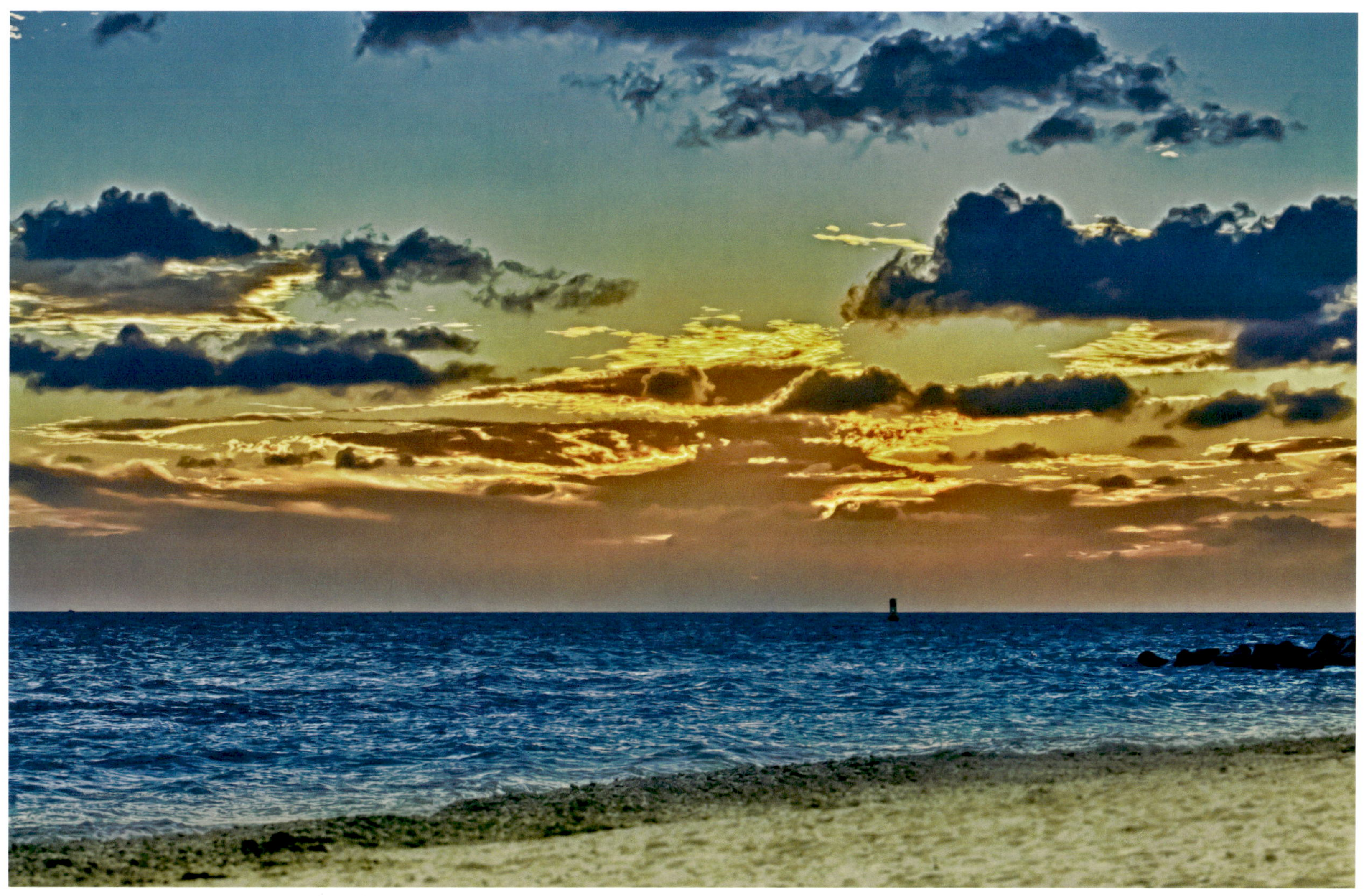

Circular Clouds Sunset: Key West Sunset at Ft. Zachary Taylor State Park on December 20, 2011. The clouds at center-left almost look like a satellite image of a hurricane.

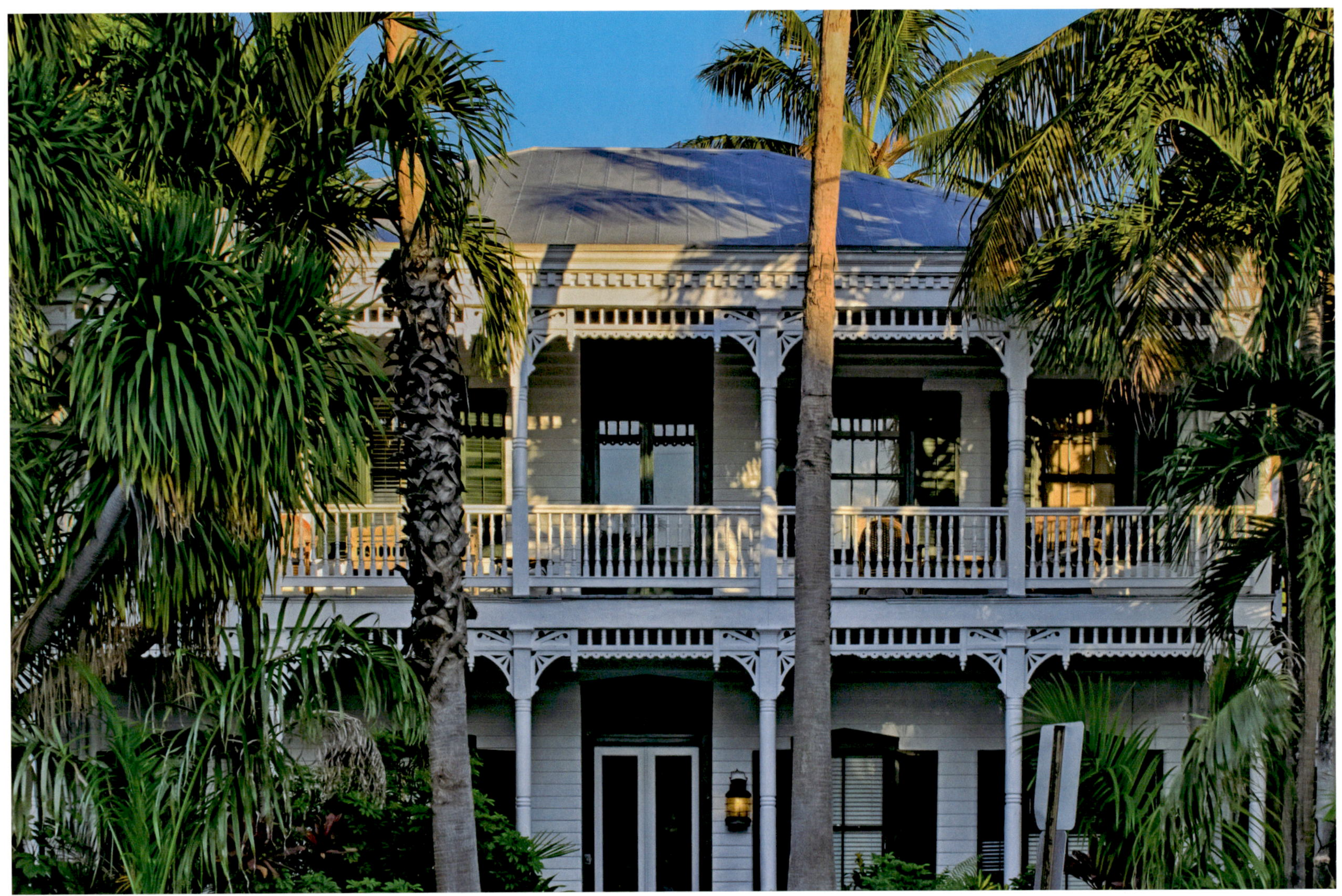

Intricate Gingerbread: A Bahama style house with wonderfully intricate gingerbread.

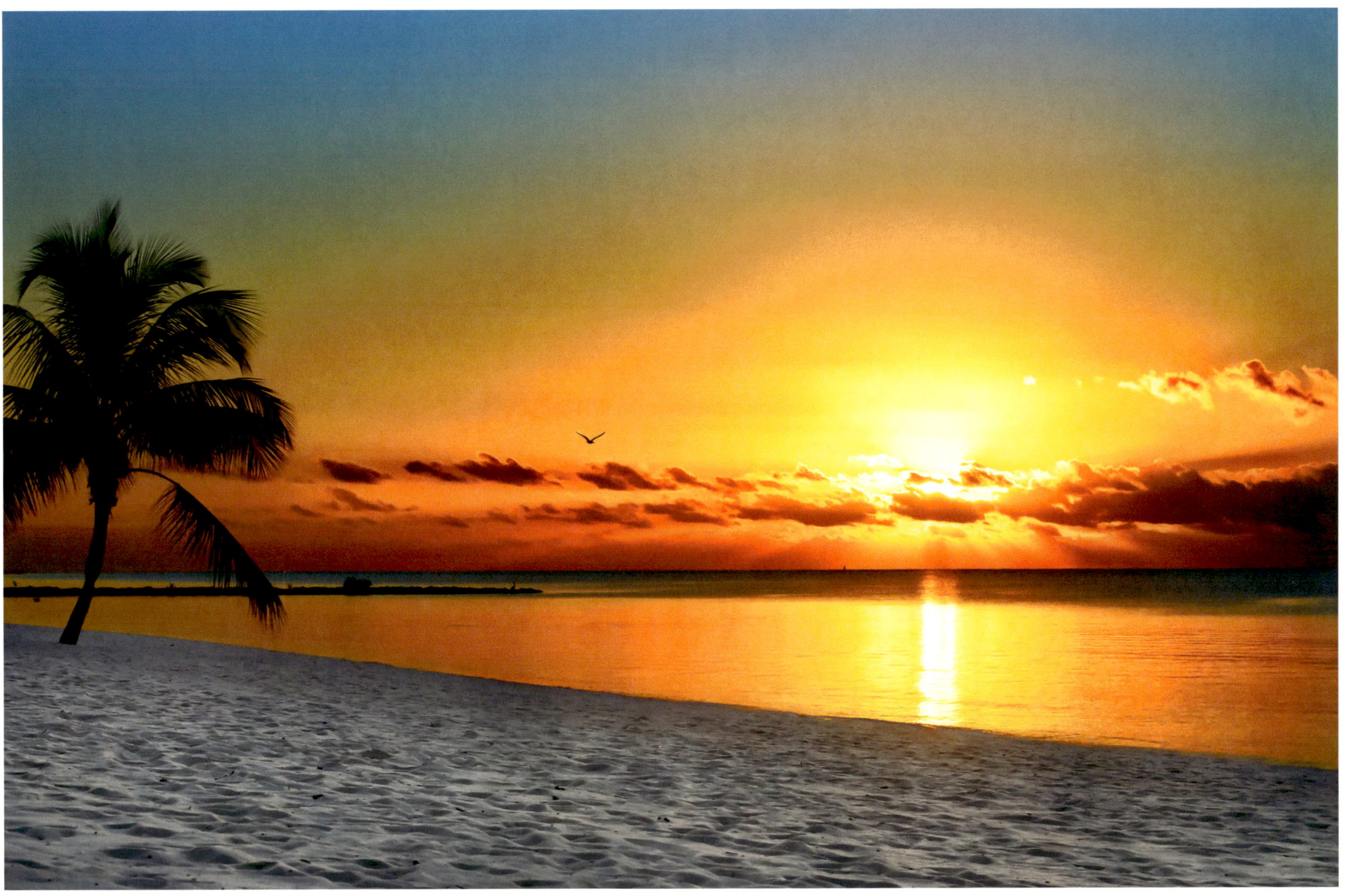

Key West Sunrise Reflection: A beautiful sunrise in Key West on November 4, 2011. It's not often the ocean is this smooth at Smathers Beach. Perfection is rare!

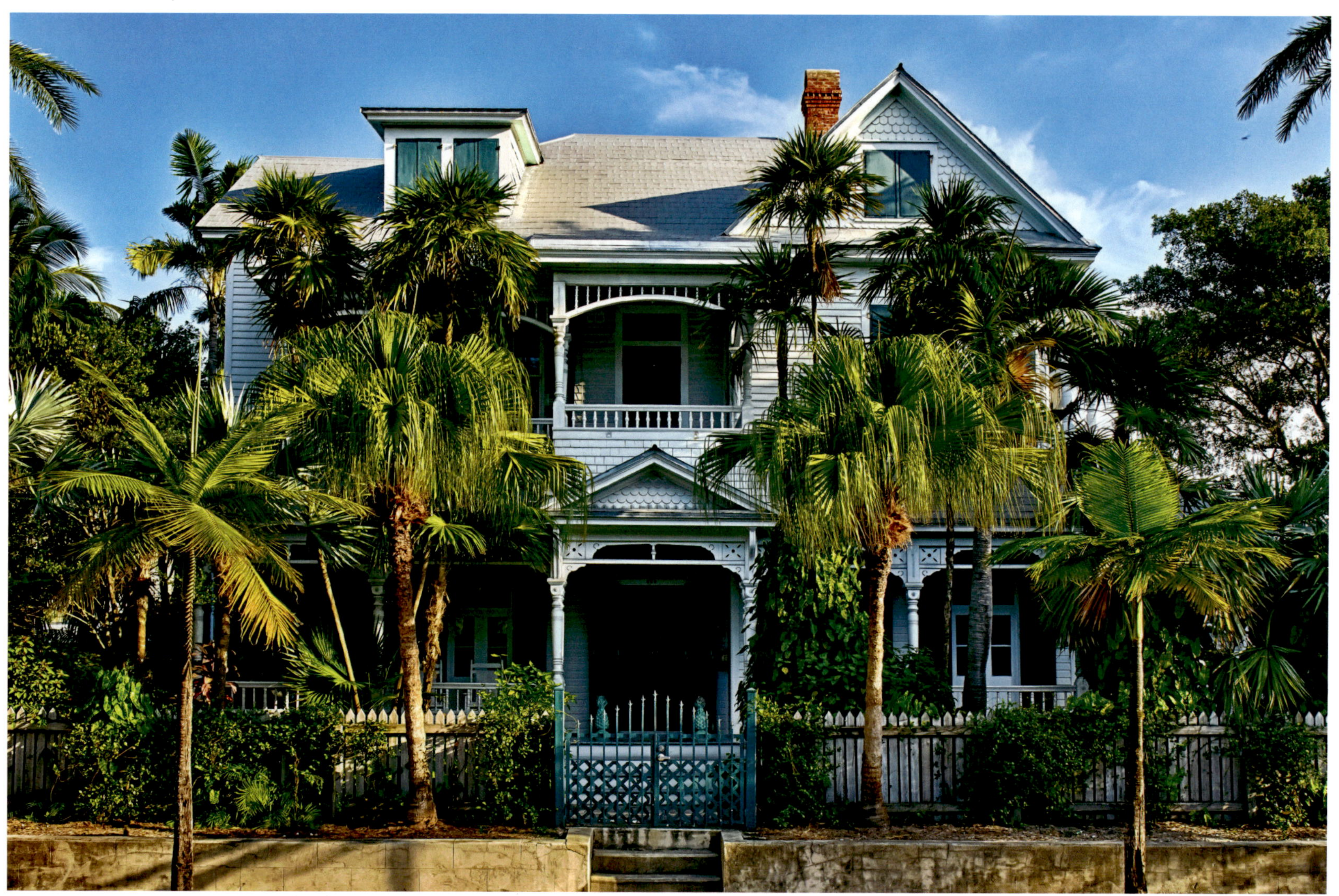

George Patterson House: George Patterson built this Queen Anne house, on Caroline Street, in 1887.

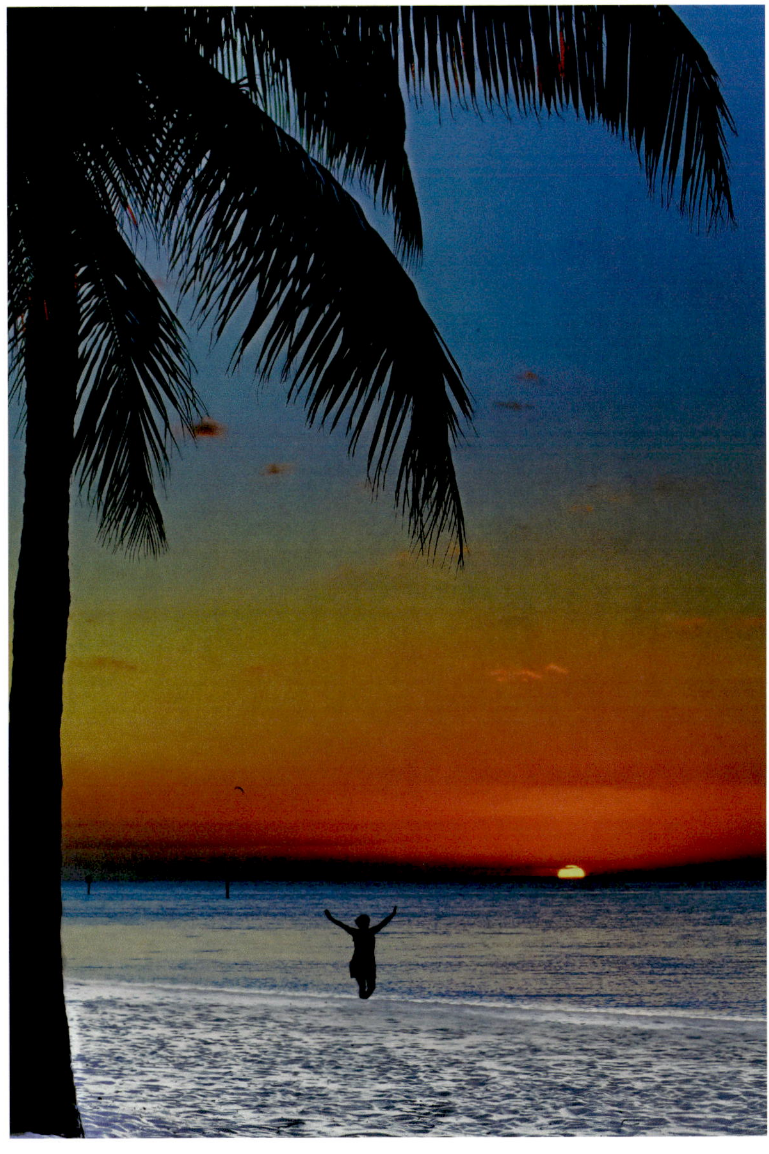

Joyful Sunrise Run: Different shades of orange accompany a sunrise run on Smathers Beach.

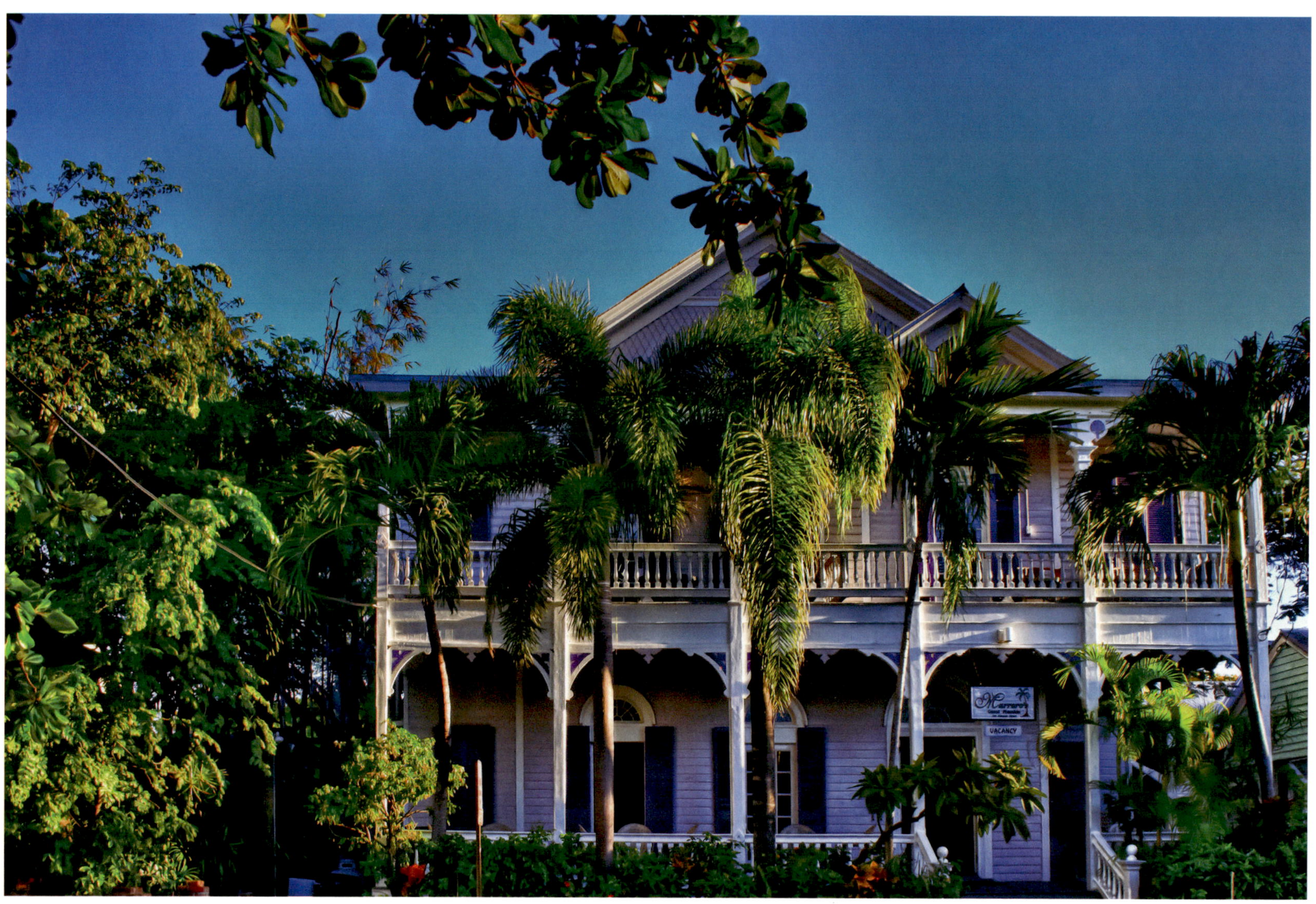

Marrero House: Francisco Marrero bribed his way out of a Cuban jail, came to Key West and by 1889 owned a large cigar factory. He built this house in the 1890's.

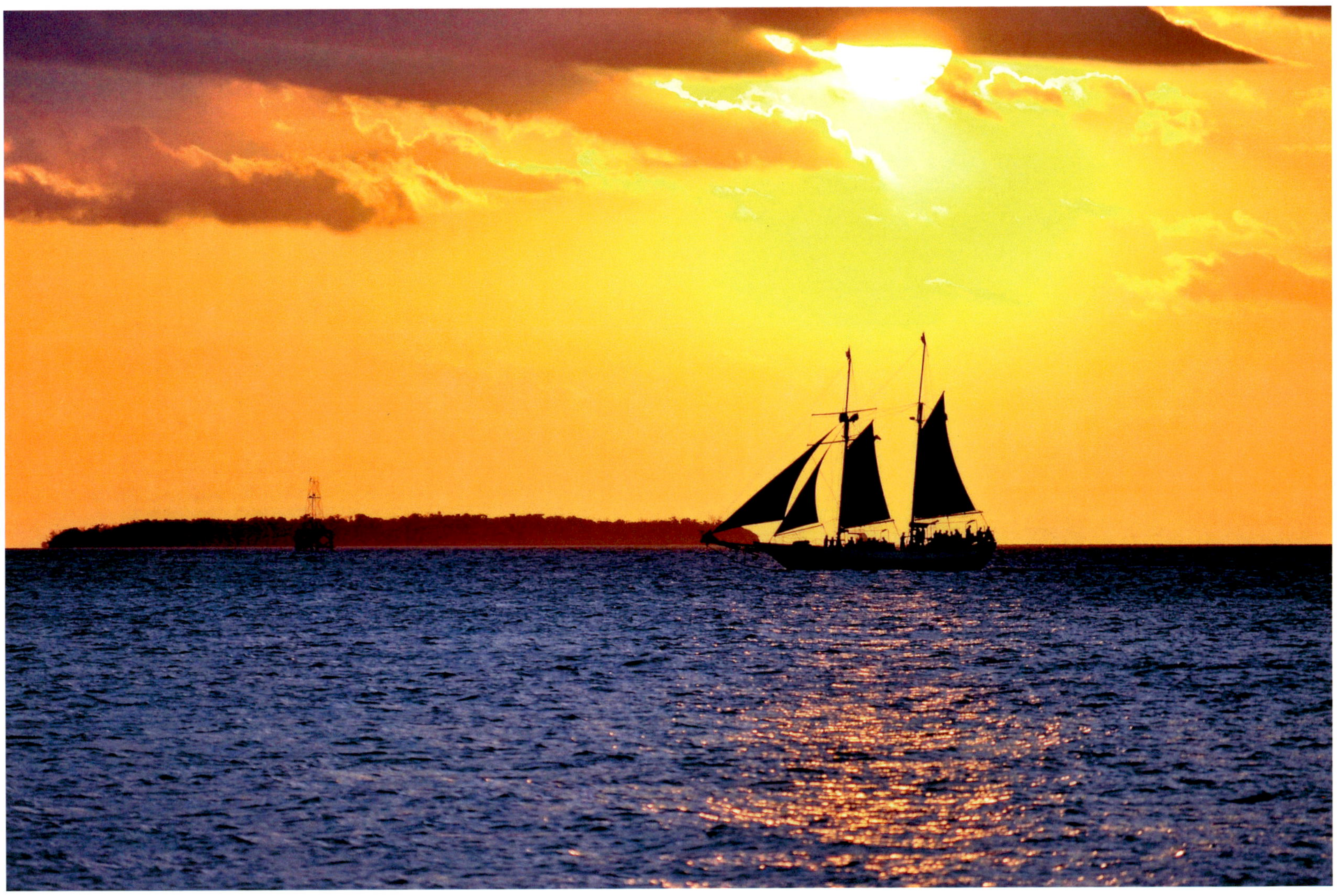

Majestic: A full rigged schooner sails by Fort Zachary Taylor at sunset on May 22, 2010.

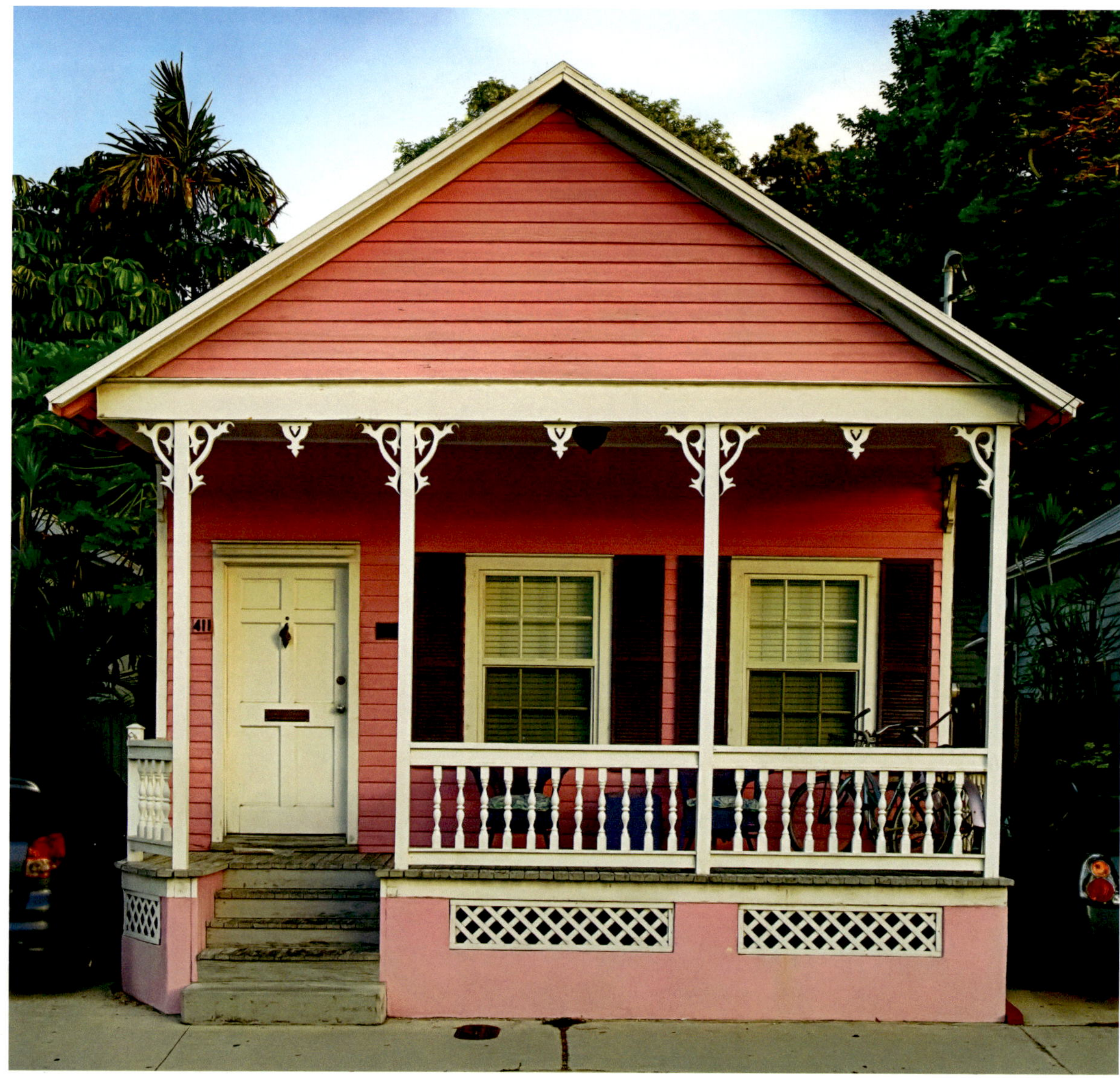

Pink Shotgun House: A Shotgun house with some nice gingerbread. Houses like this were built all over Key West in the 1880's for the cigar factory workers.

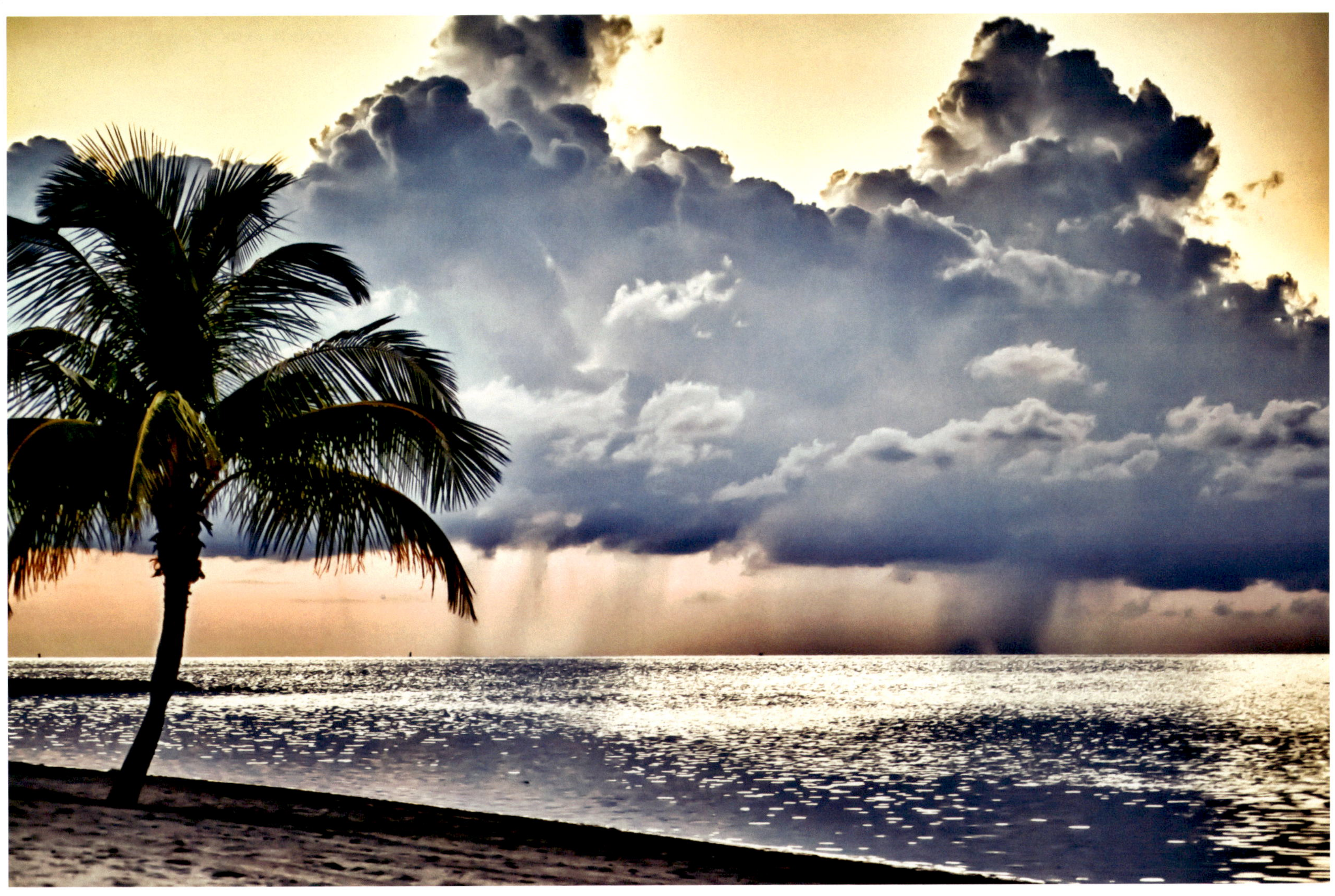

Morning Rain: The distant rain casts a unique, lavender hue on Smathers Beach.

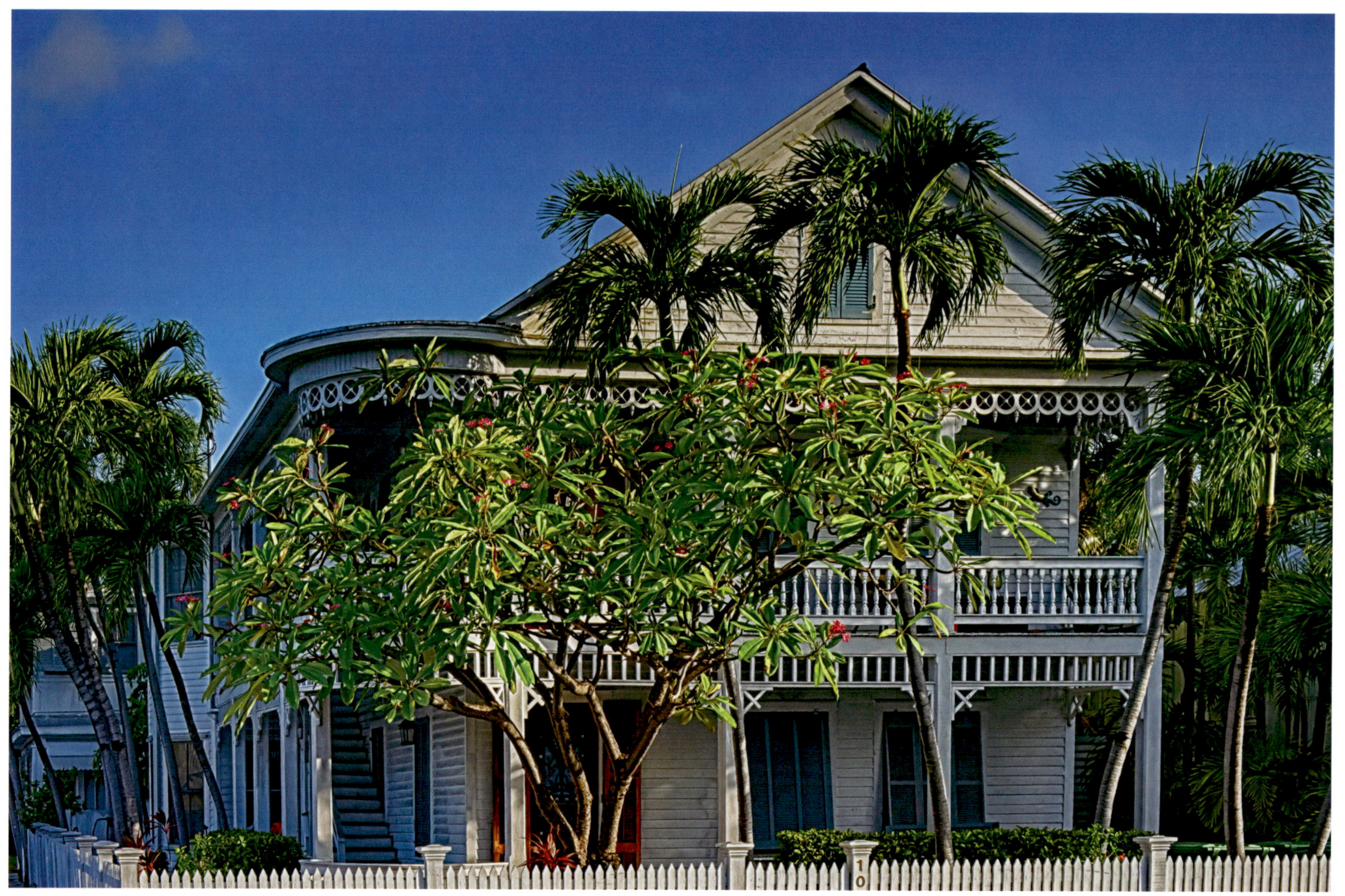

Ship Wheel Gingerbread: Benito Alfonso built this house in 1891. In 1906 Antonio Diaz y Carrasco, the first Cuban Consul to the United States, bought this house and his consul office was here.

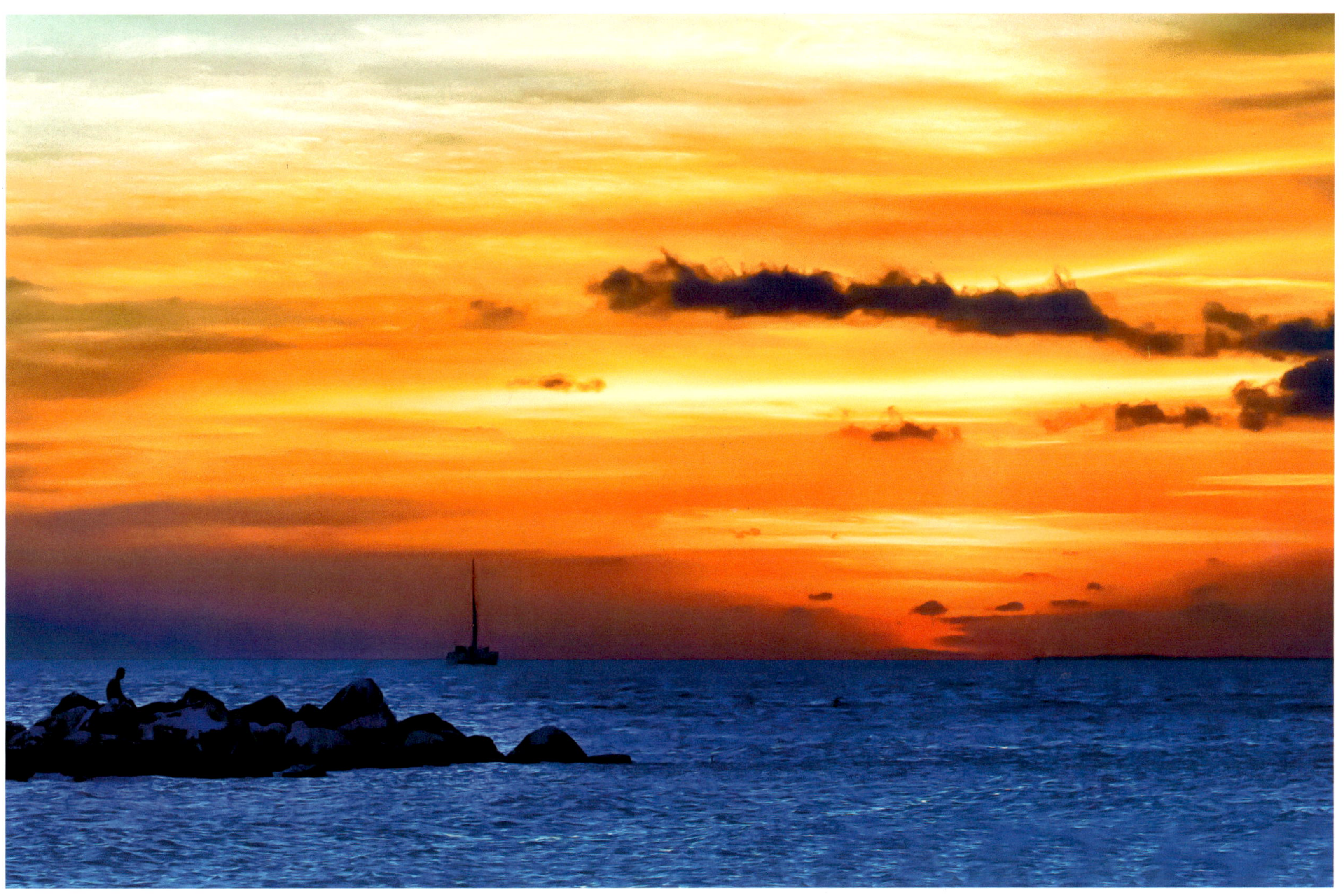

Secluded Sunset: A man marvels at the colors after a completely unique, fabulous Key West sunset.

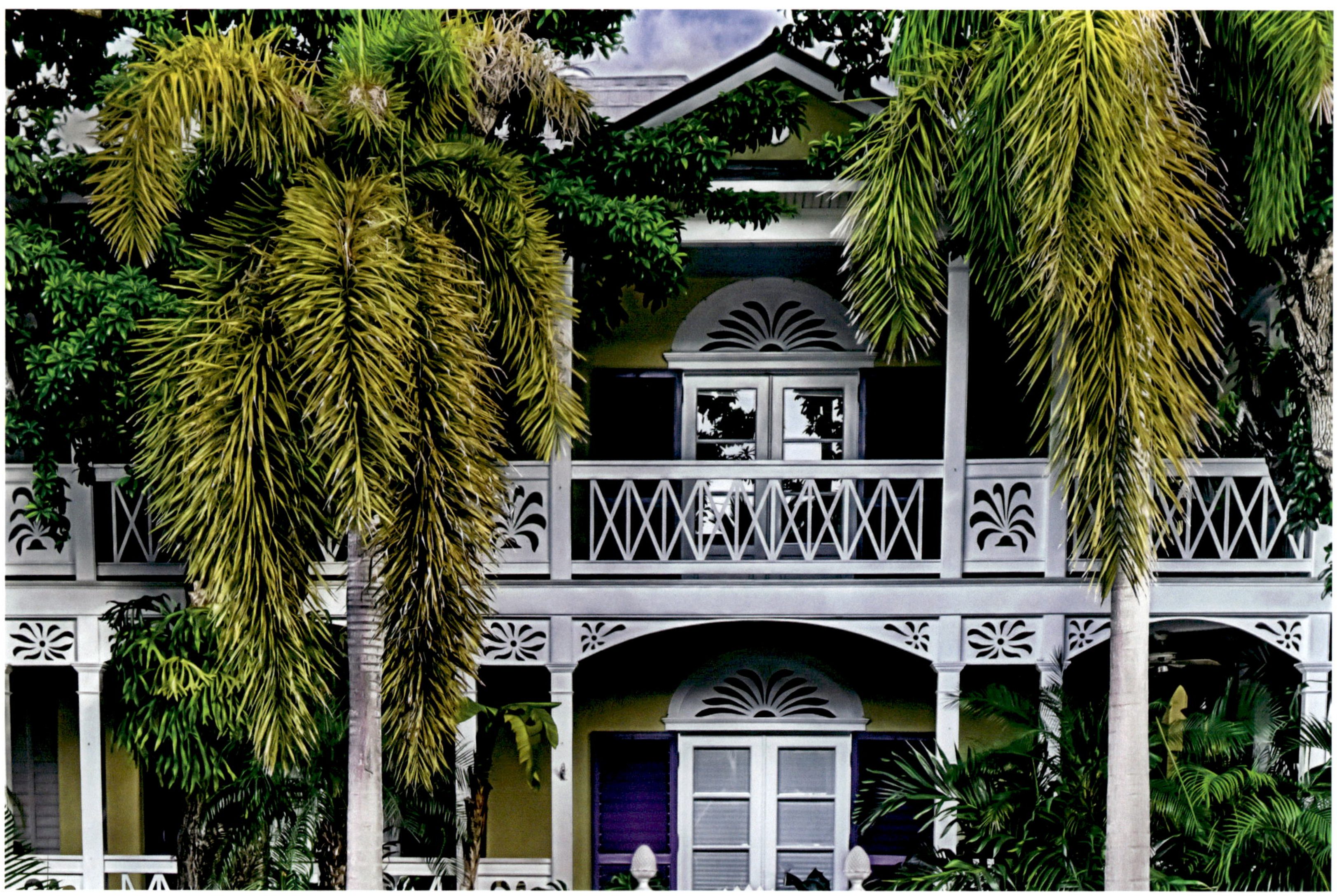

Key West Classic: This is one of the finest homes in Old Town.

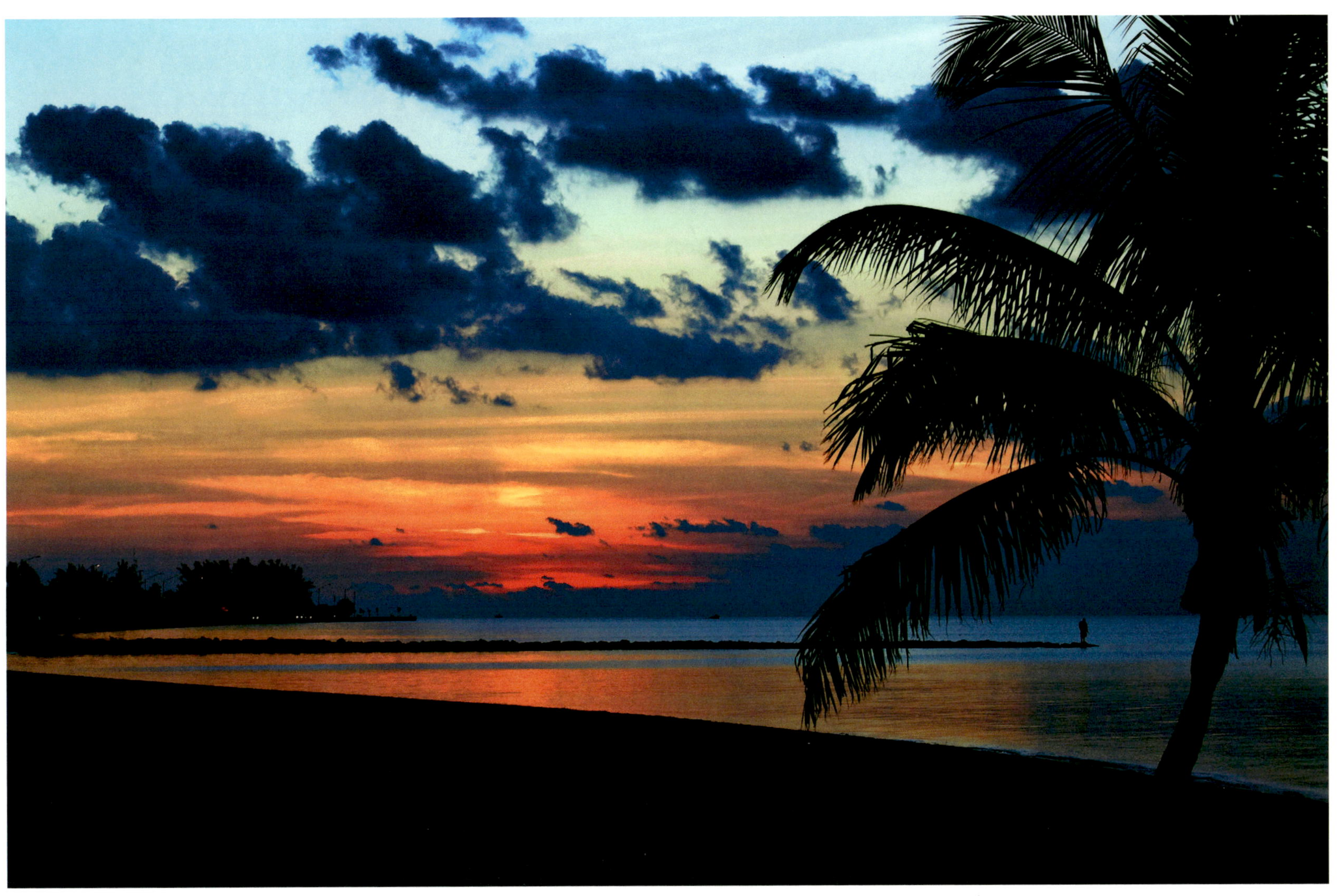

Key West Sunrise Palm: A beautiful, calm sunrise on October 3, 2010. The range of colors, from light blue at the top to the deep red at the horizon, and the corresponding reflection, make this sunrise incredibly unique.

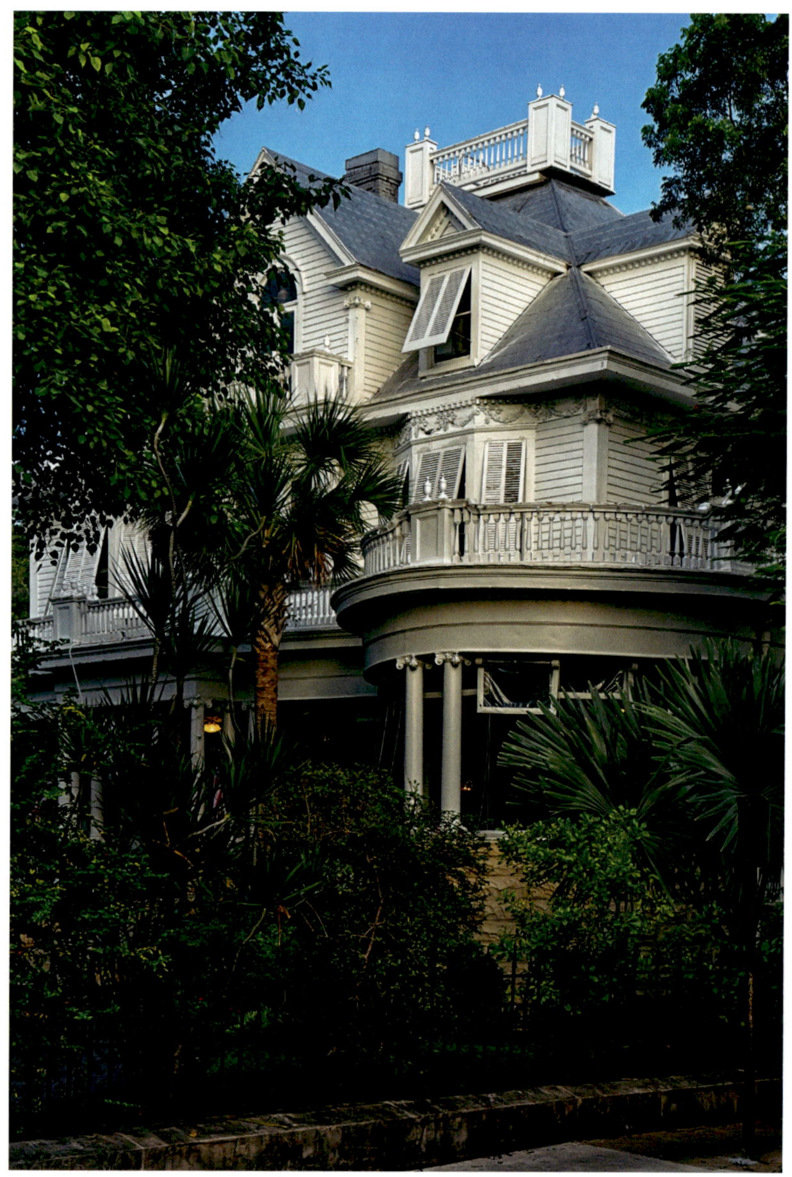

Curry Mansion: Built by Milton Curry in 1905, this house is in the Newport Cottage style that was popular in the late 1800's.

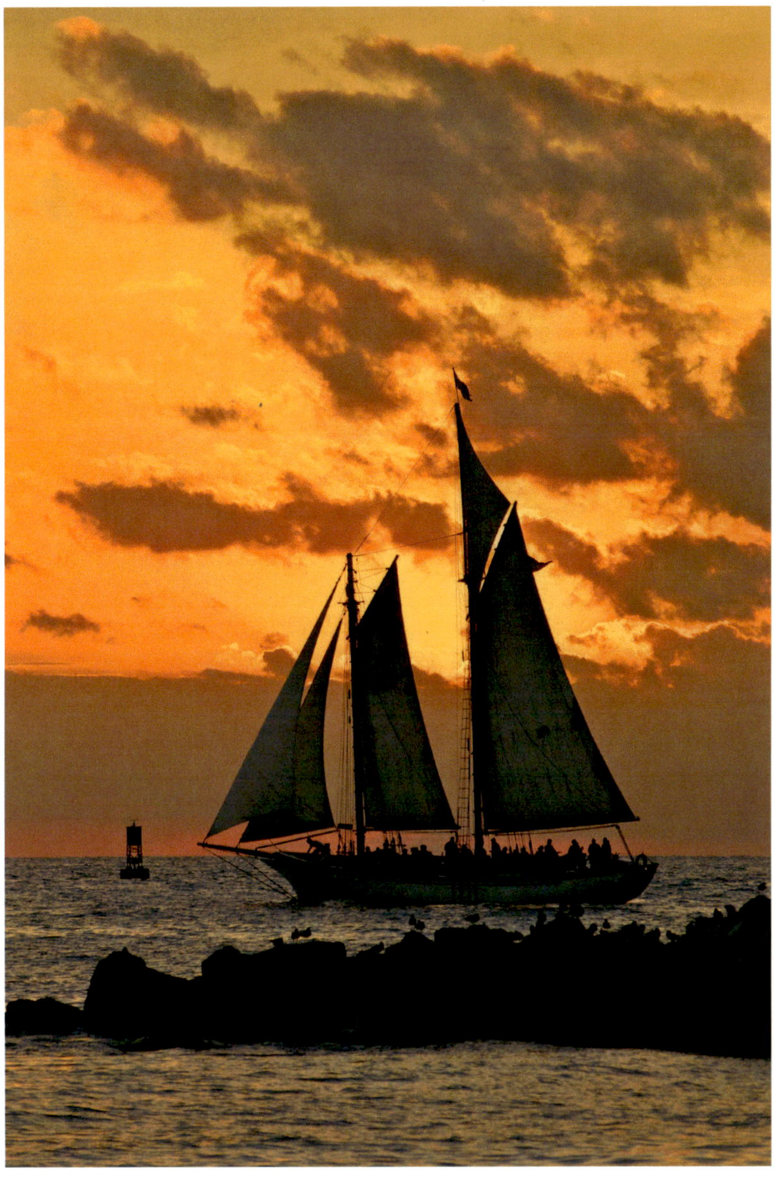

Hidden Sun Sail: A full rigged schooner compliments the Key West sunset.

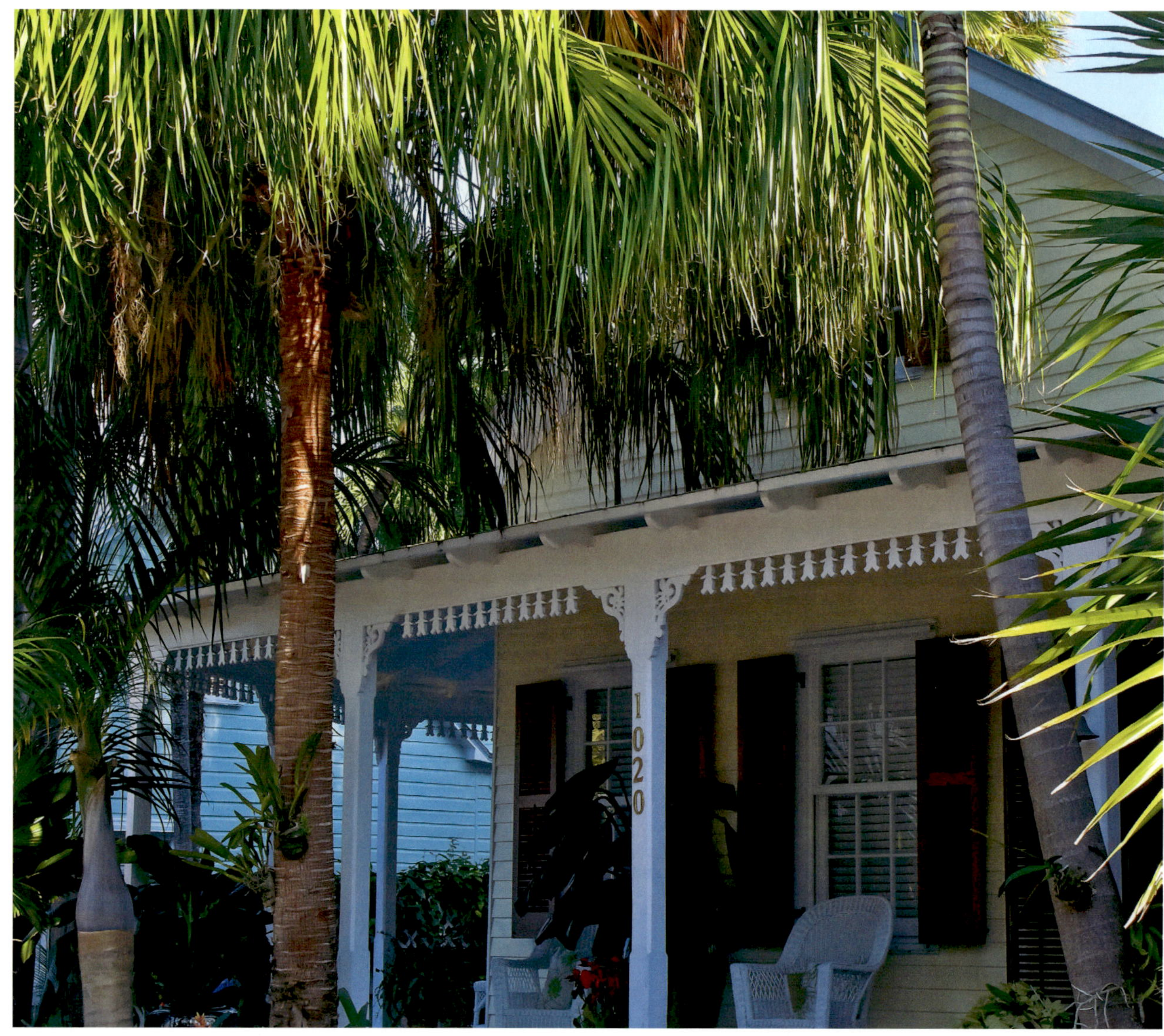

Gingerbread Men: One of the most popular houses in Old Town: Gingerbread Men gingerbread!

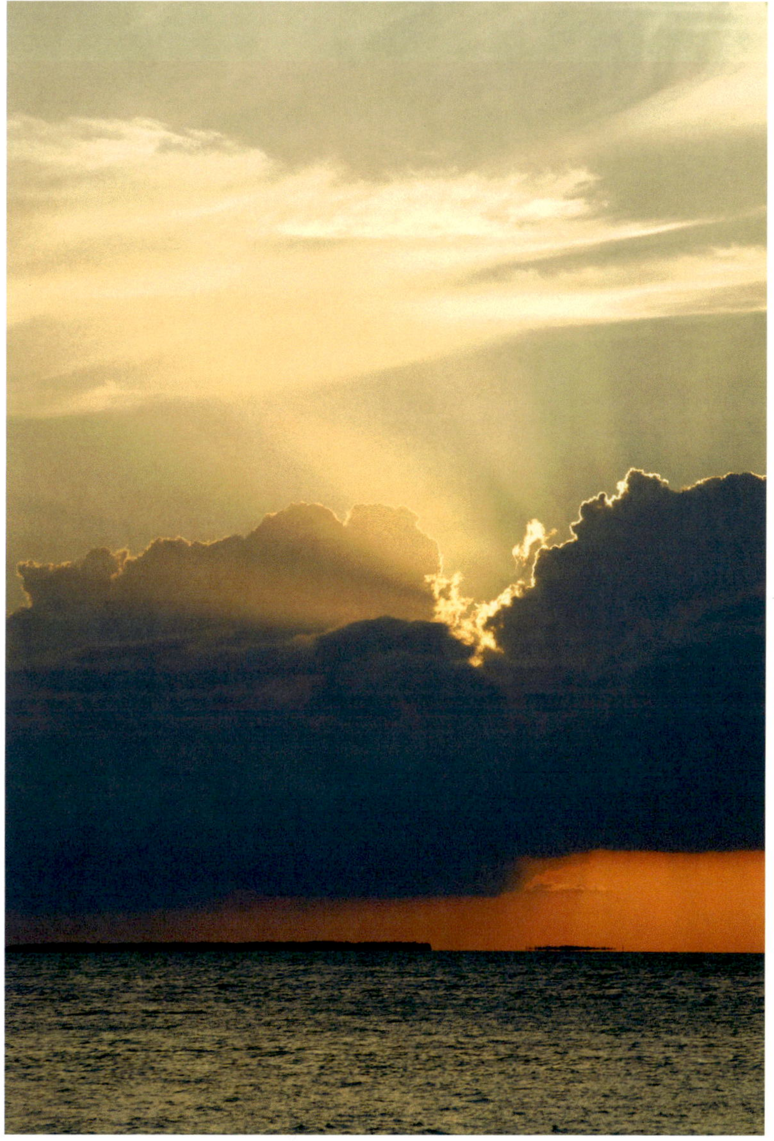

Sun Rays: A magnificent view as the sun's rays, behind the dark clouds, divide the colors and the brightness of the scene. Shot on May 5, 2011 on South Roosevelt Boulevard.

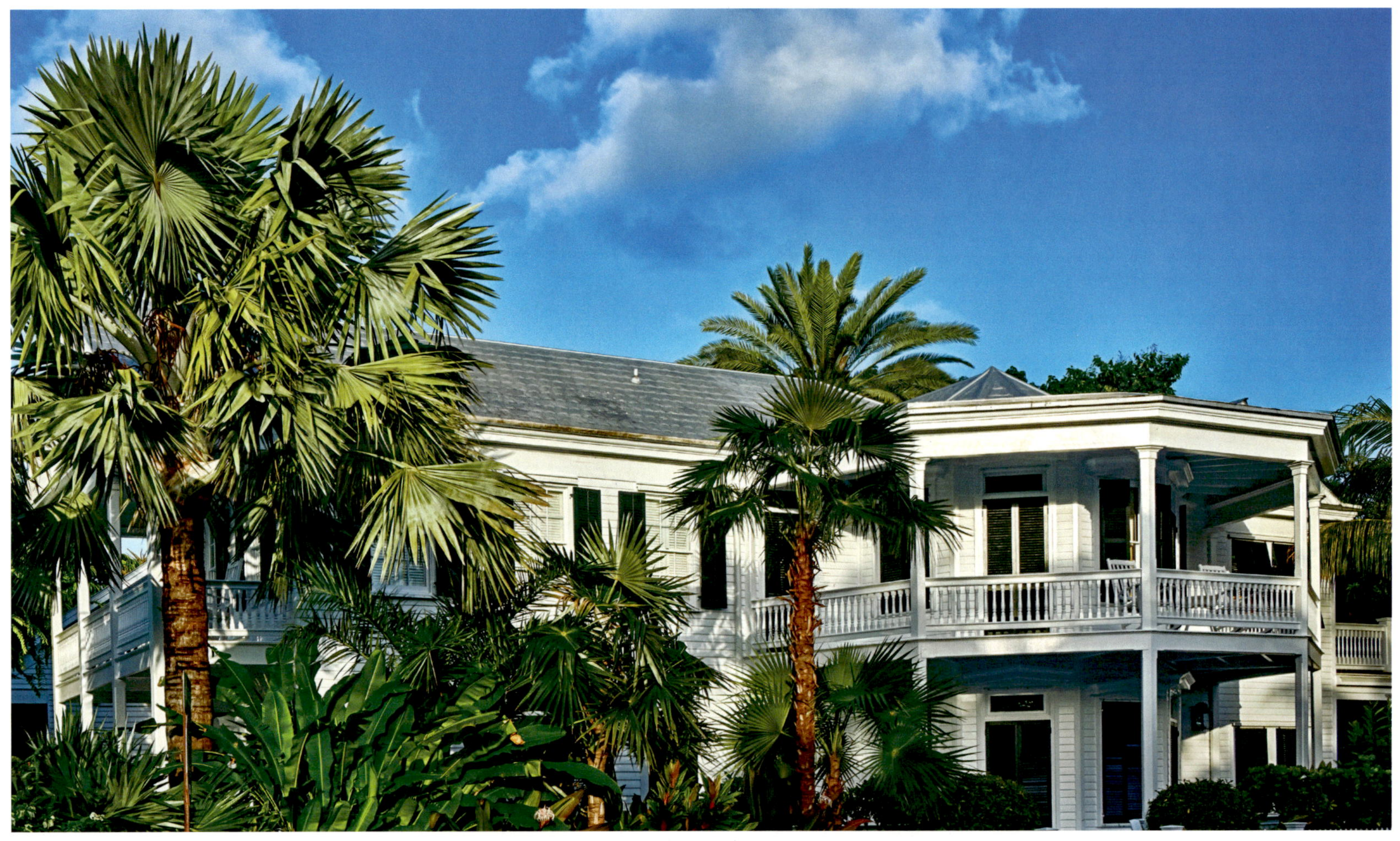

Norberg Thompson House: Thomas Thompson built this house in 1880. His son, Norberg founded Thompson Enterprises, builders of the schooner "Western Union."

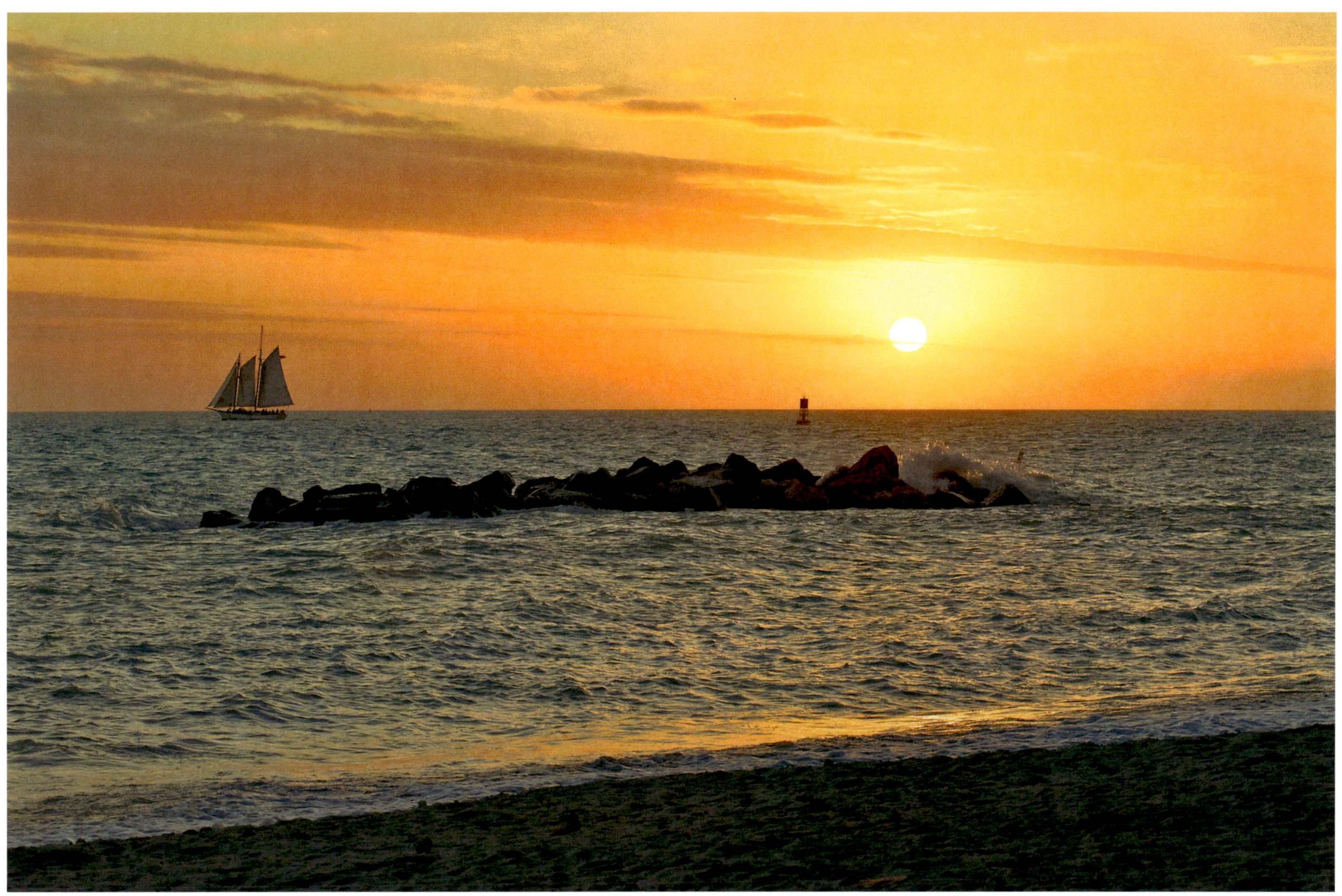

Headed South: A full rigged schooner heads south on the last day of 2010.

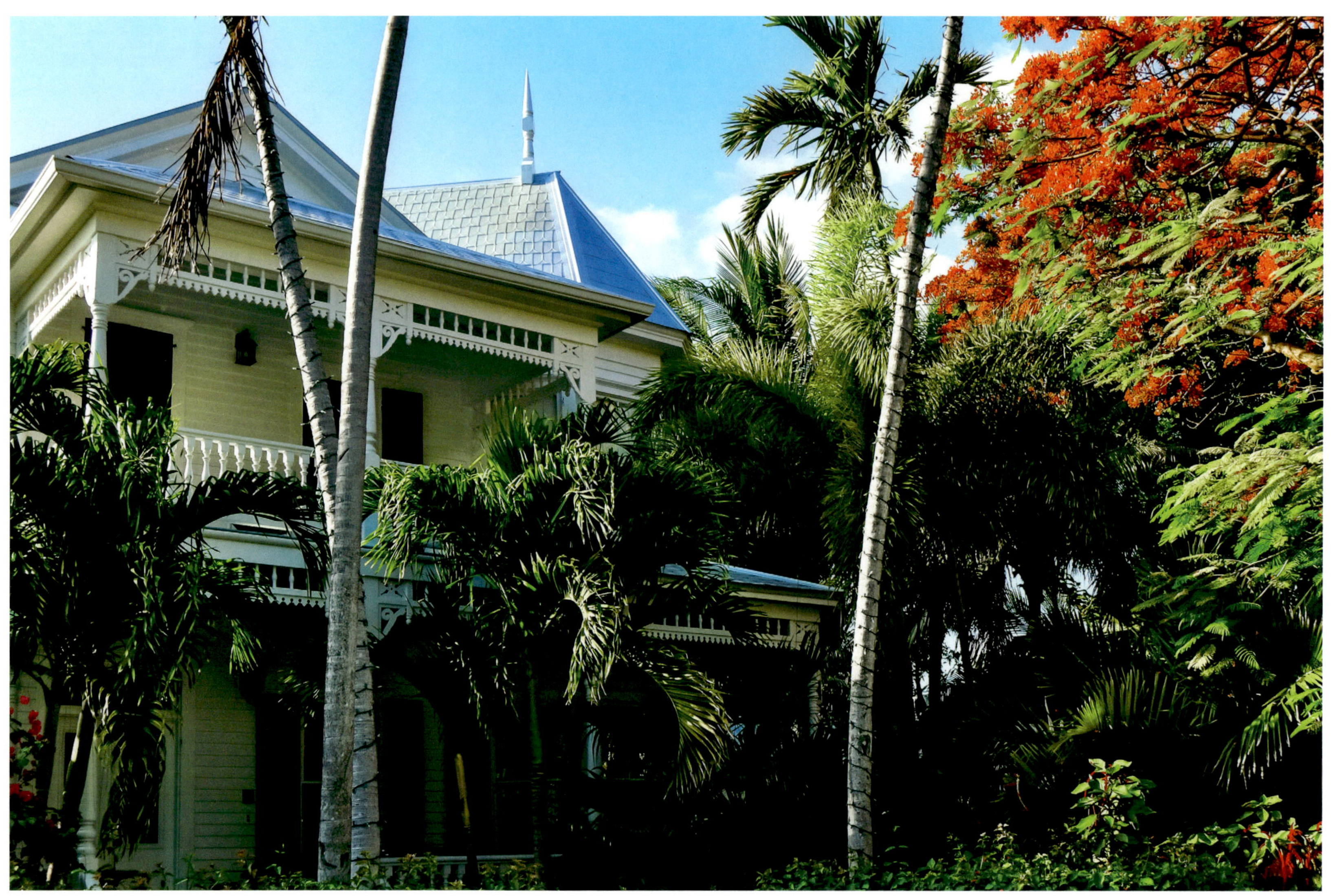

Conch House: A Victorian gingerbread house with a beautiful Royal Poinciana tree on Southard Street.

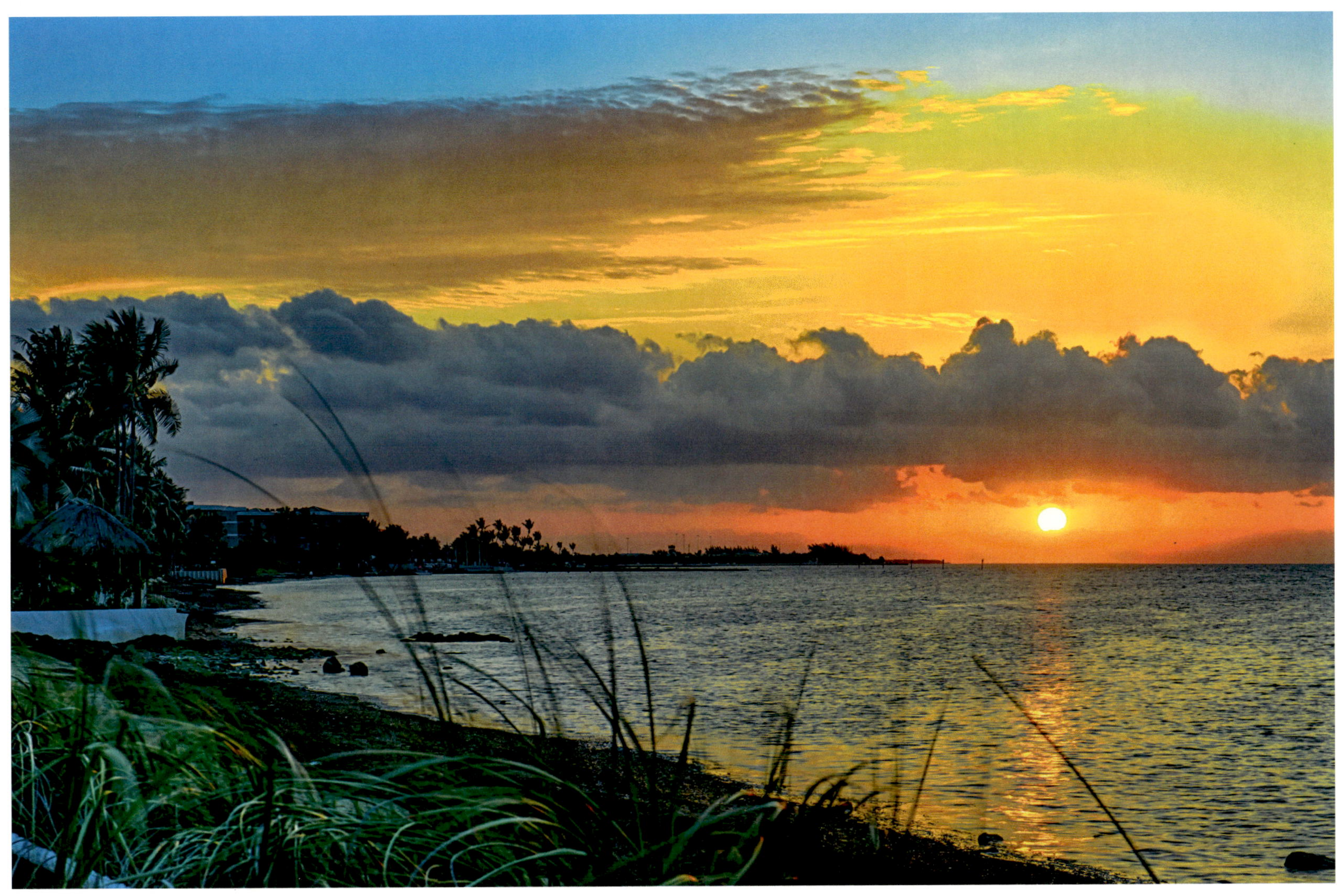

Coastline Sunrise: The Key West coastline as seen from C.B. Harvey Park on March 31, 2013.

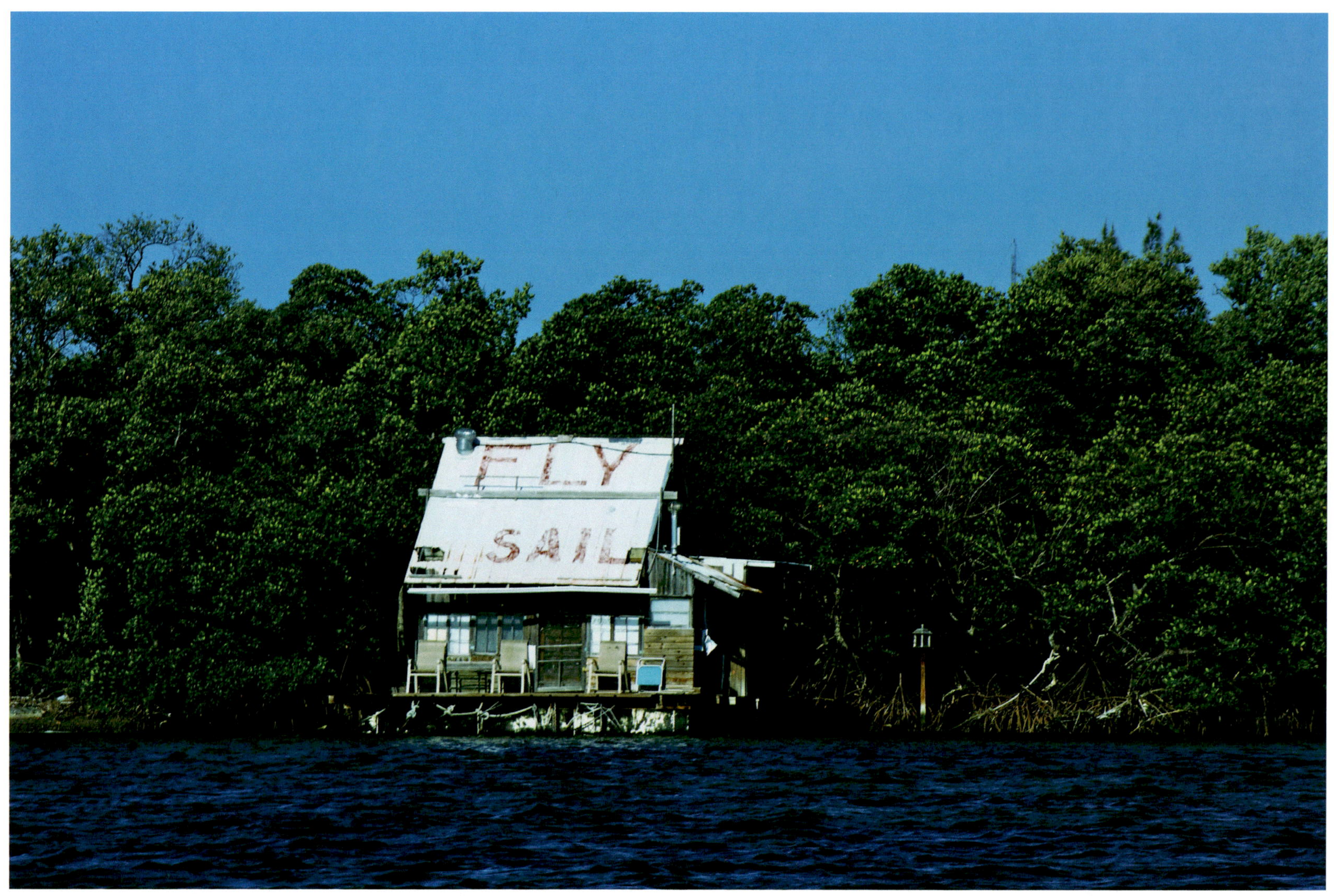

Fly Sail Shack: Shot offshore of Big Pine, Florida on April 22, 2011.

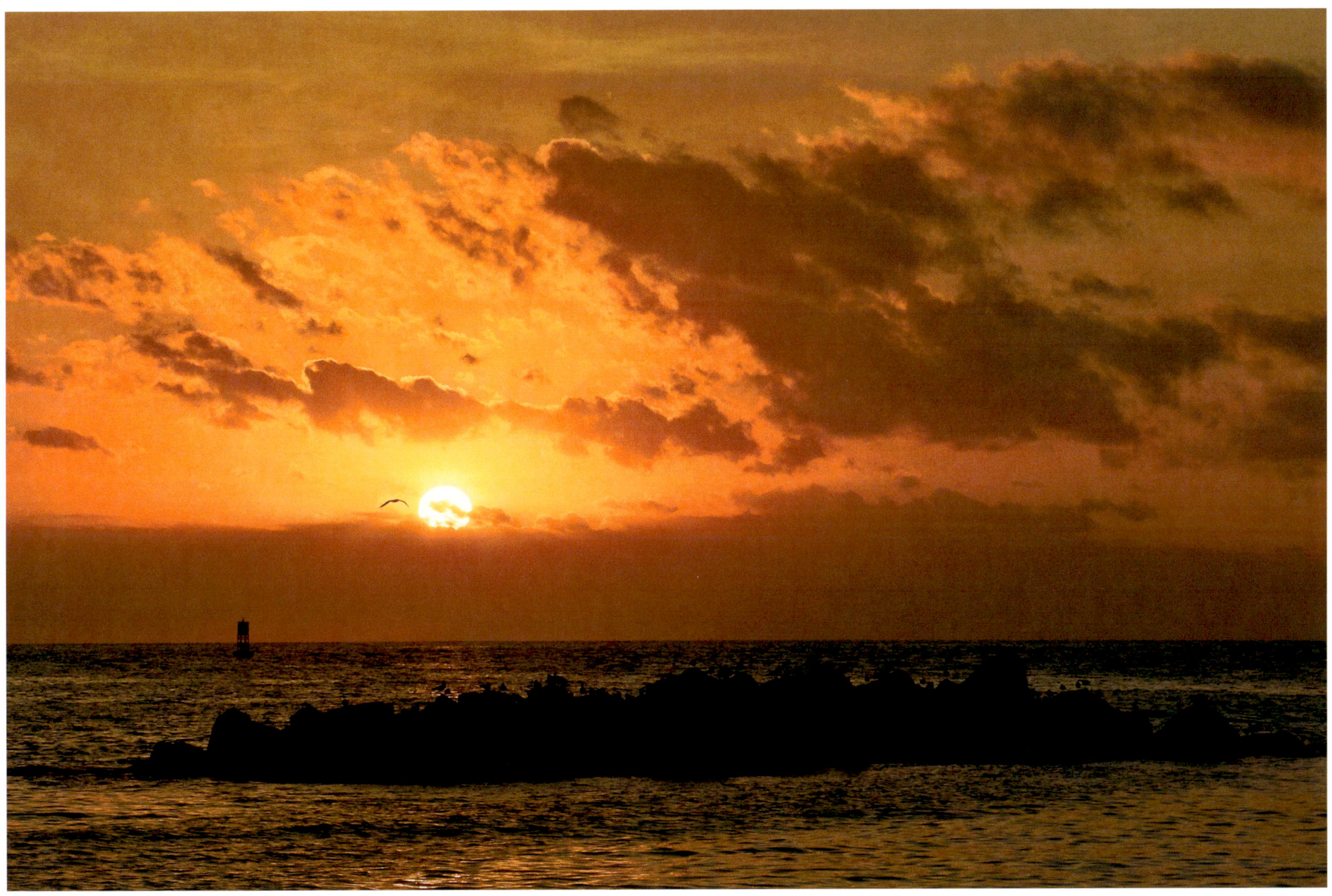

Clouds on Fire: The dark rocks in the ocean emphasize the explosion of light on January 7, 2011.

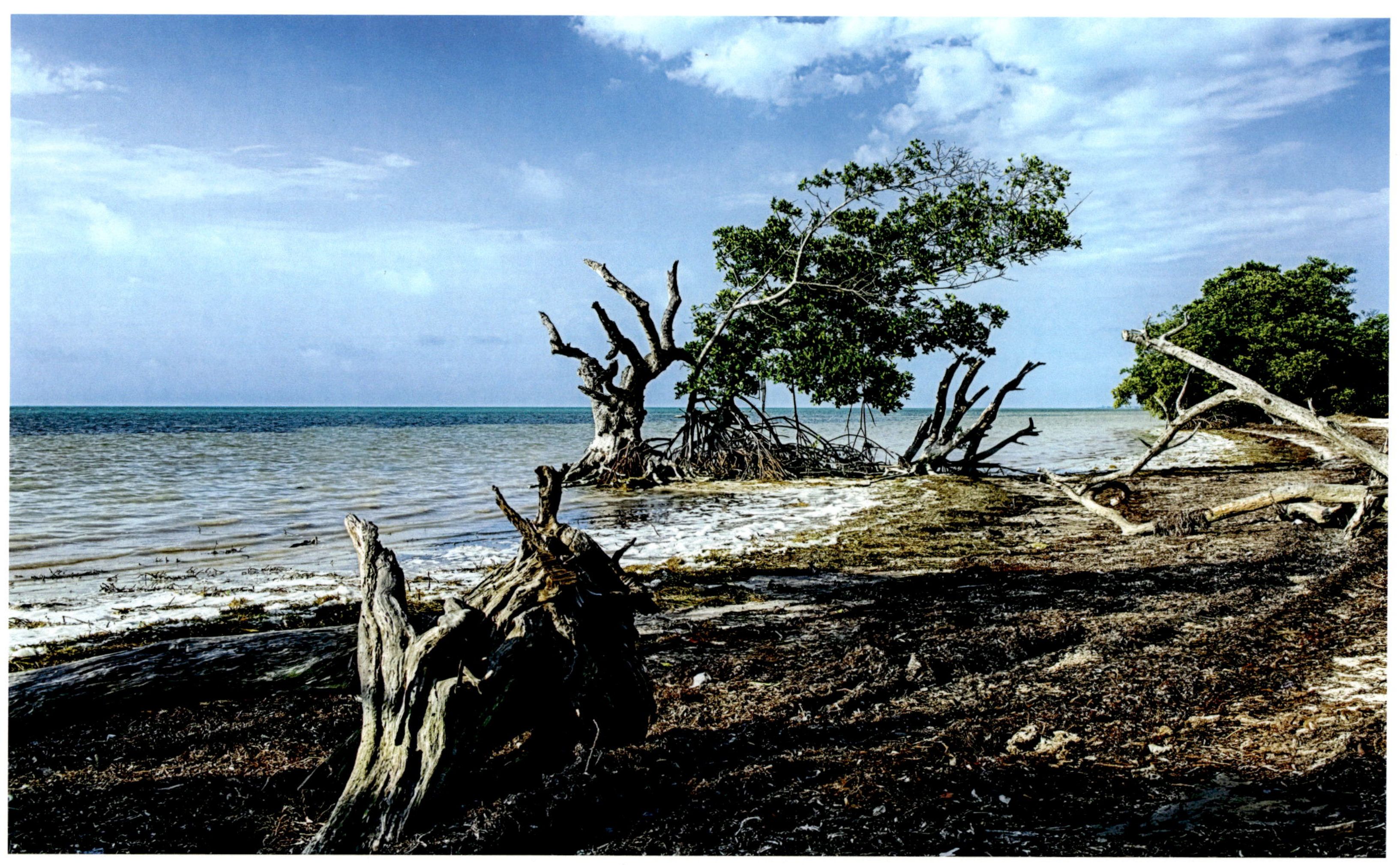

Re-Birth: A mangrove tree in the magnificent Florida Keys, on the morning of February 23, 2013.

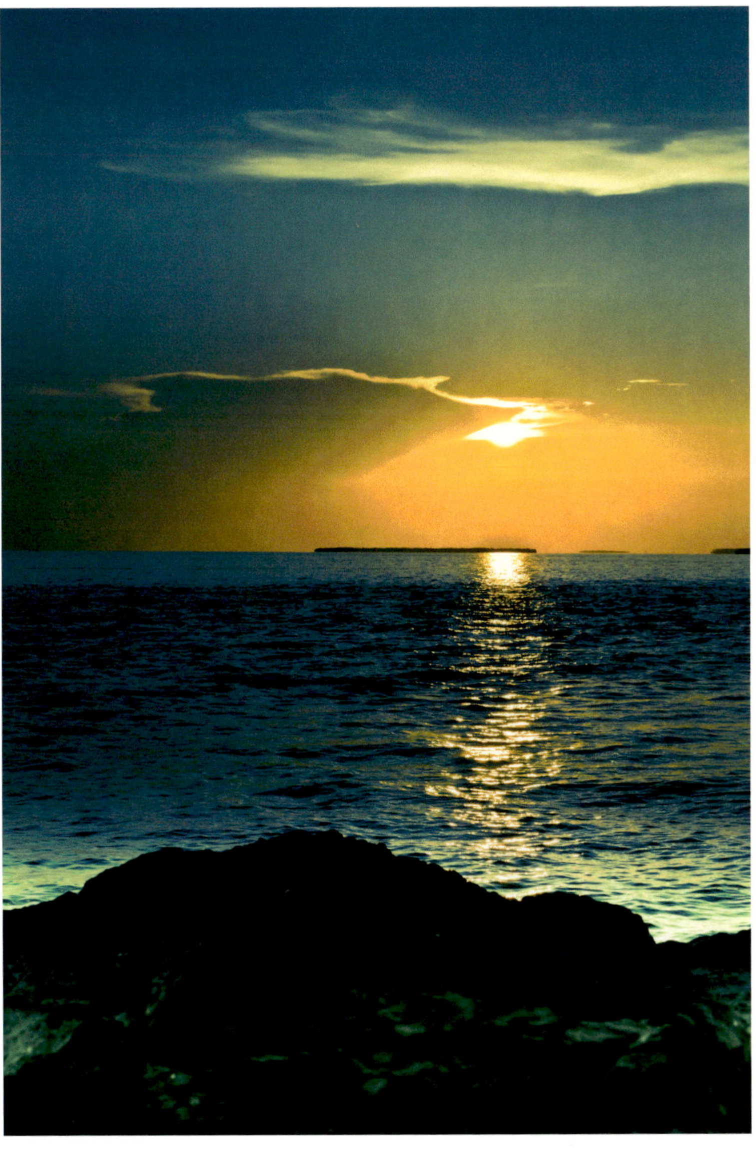

Rocky Sunset: The rocks at Ft. Zachary Taylor State Park and the ocean reflect the sunset, as the colors of the ocean modulate.

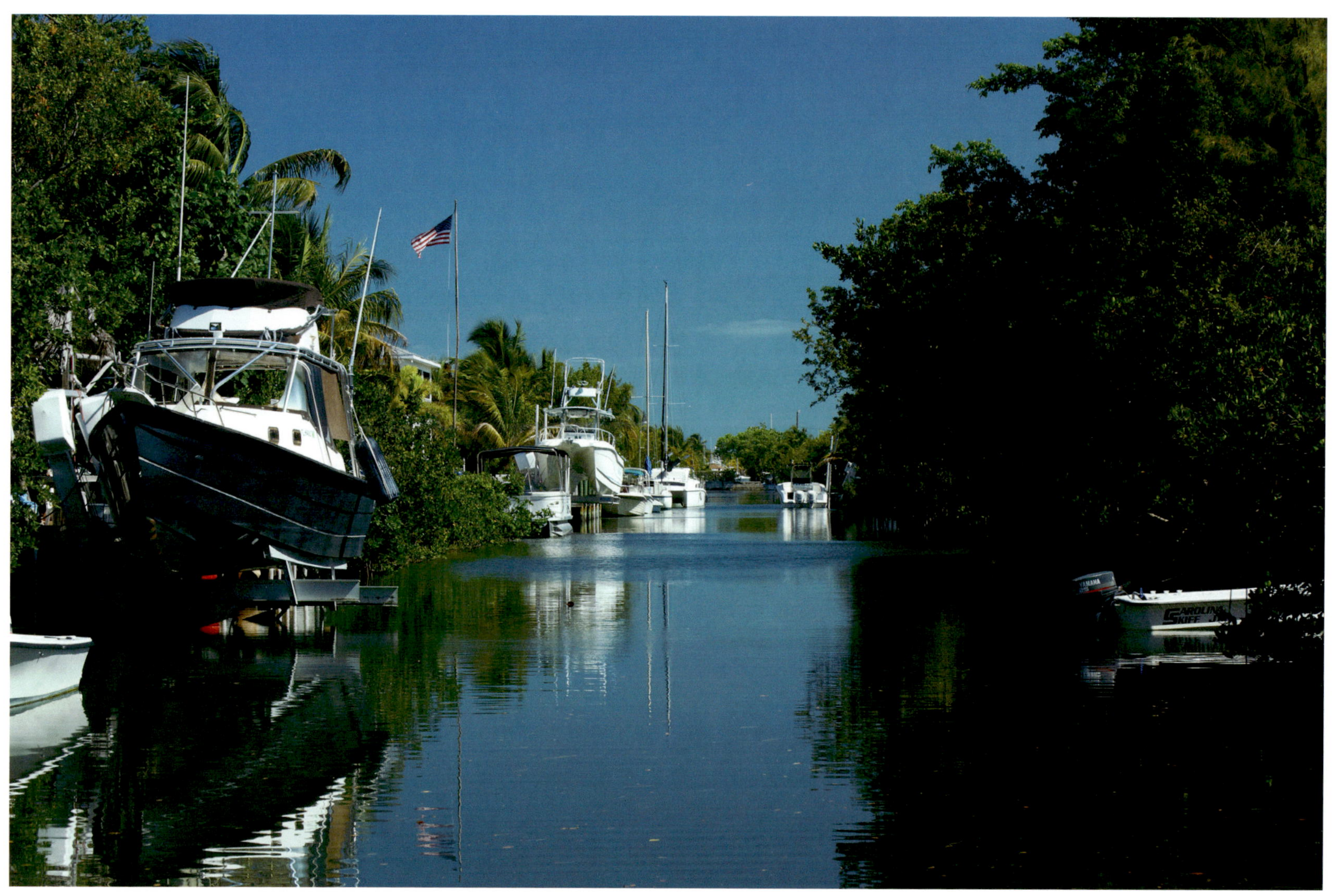

Stormy's Driveway: We're headed for Stormy's house! Shot in Big Pine, Florida on April 22, 2011.

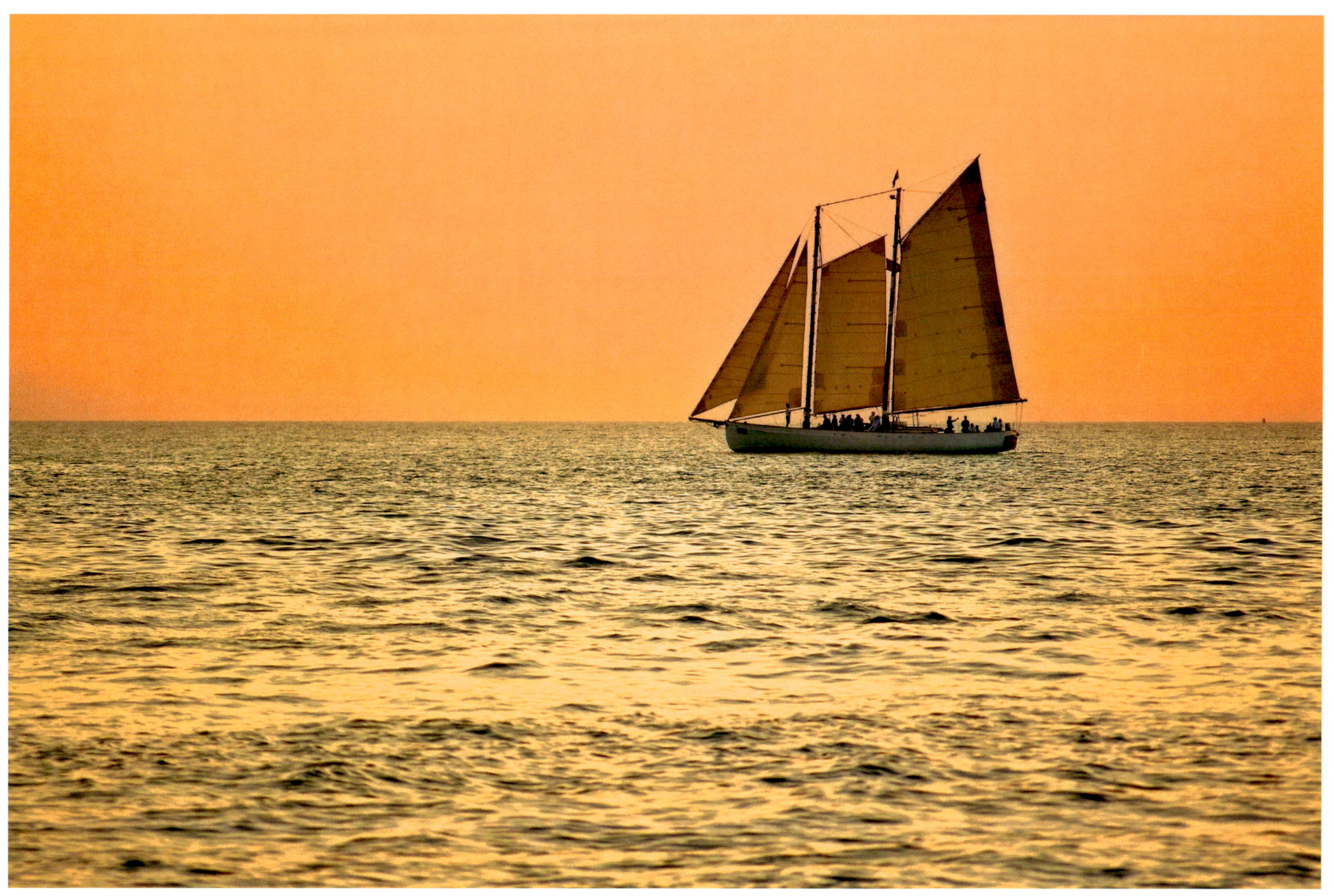

Orange Sky: A schooner enjoys the calm water of Key West on January 31, 2011.

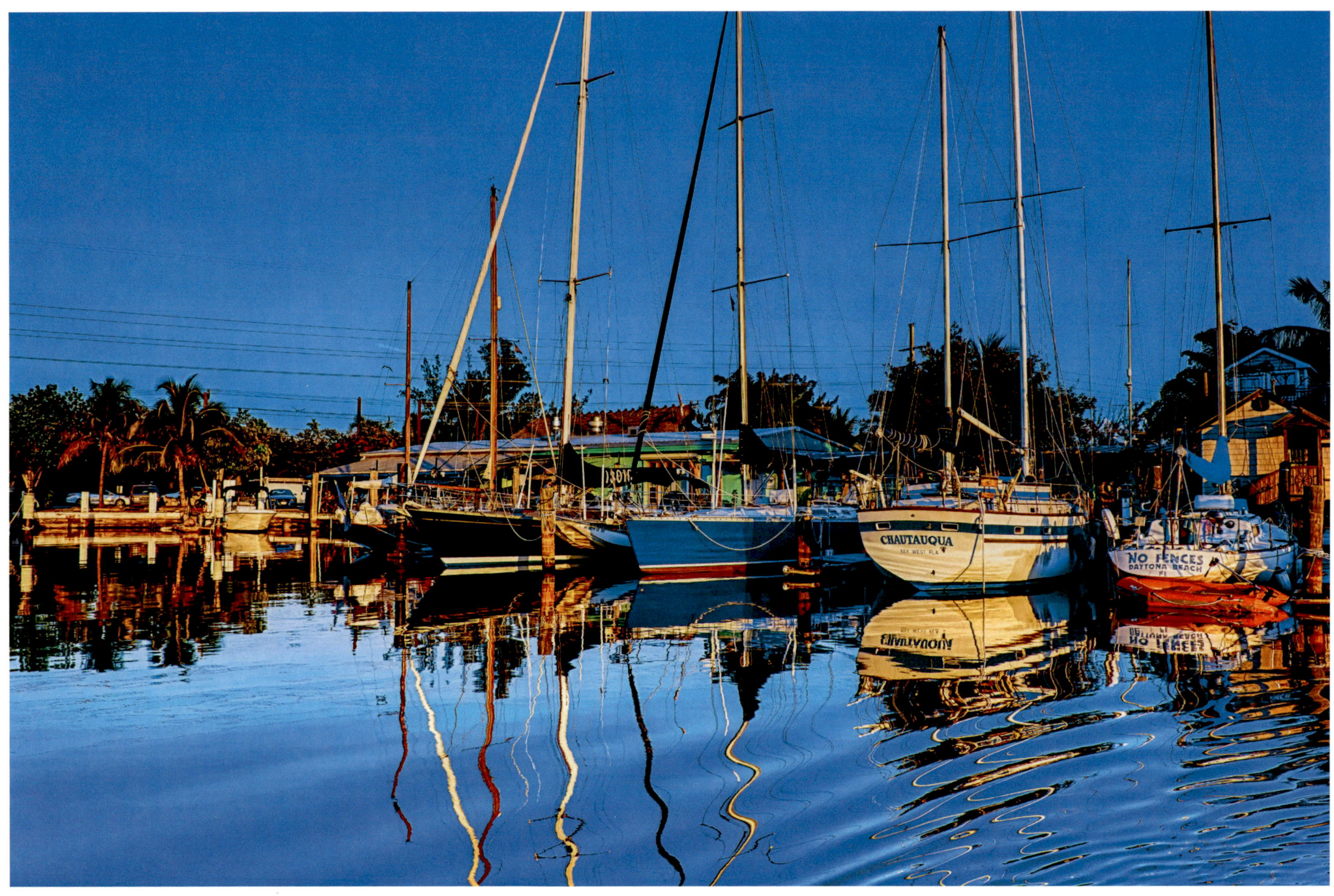

Safe Harbor Reflection: A few boats docked at Safe Harbor reflect the beauty of the spectacular Florida Keys.

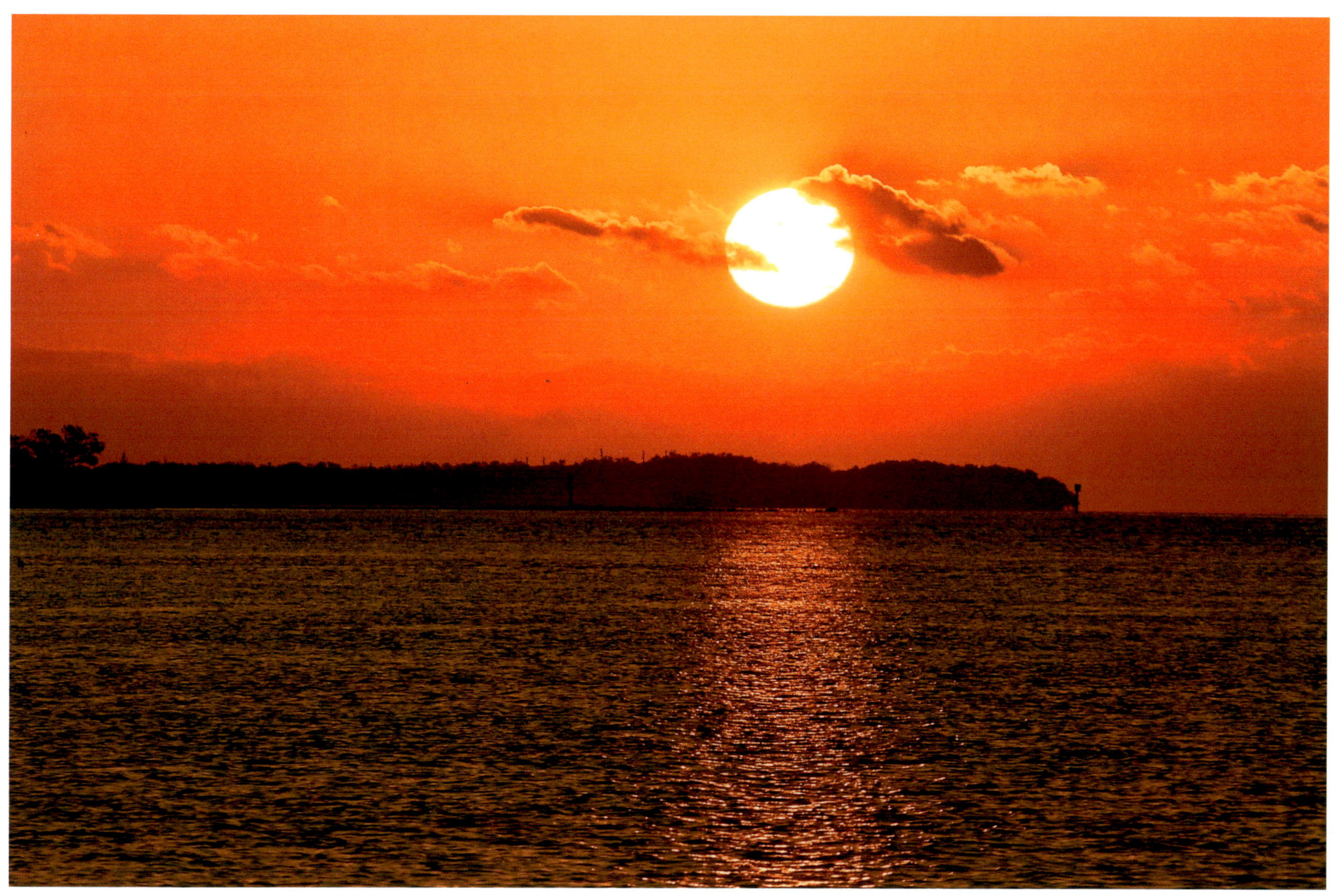

A Bite from the Sun: The clouds take a bite from the sun. All of the different shades of orange are amazing!

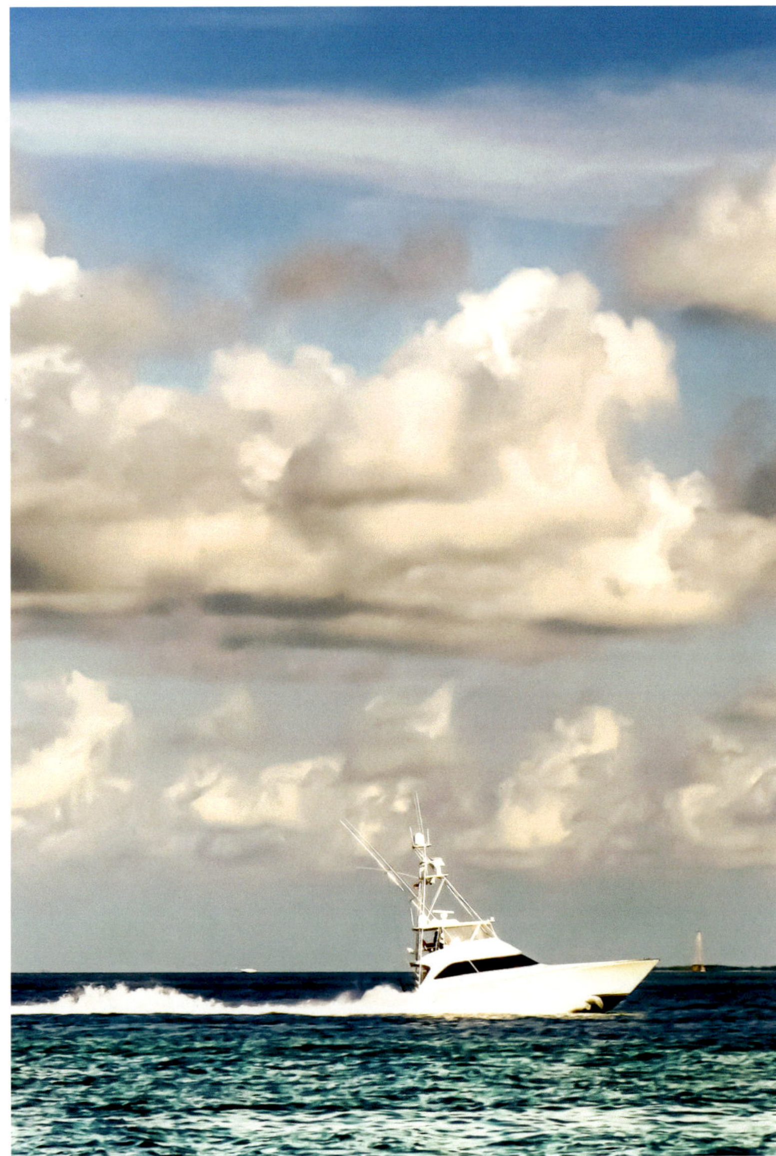

First to the Fish: A Sport Fisher races out to begin another glorious day in Key West.

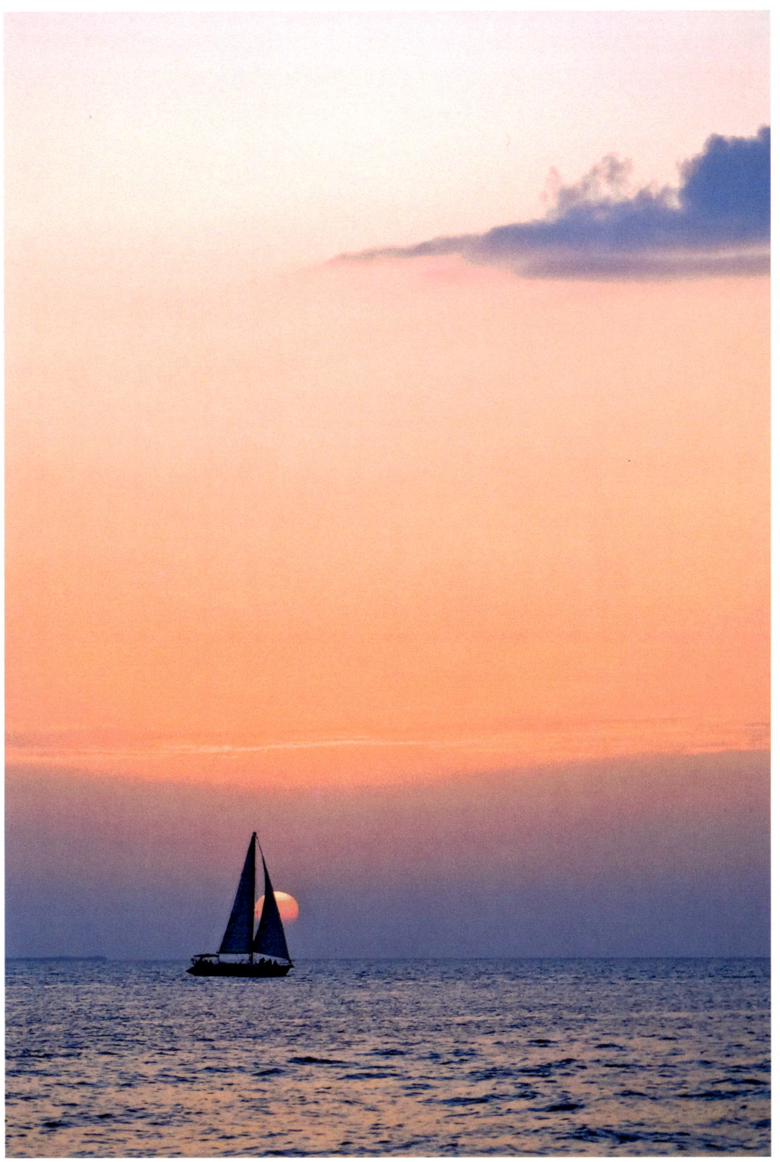

Sunset Pink: A sloop sails into a serene pink sunset.

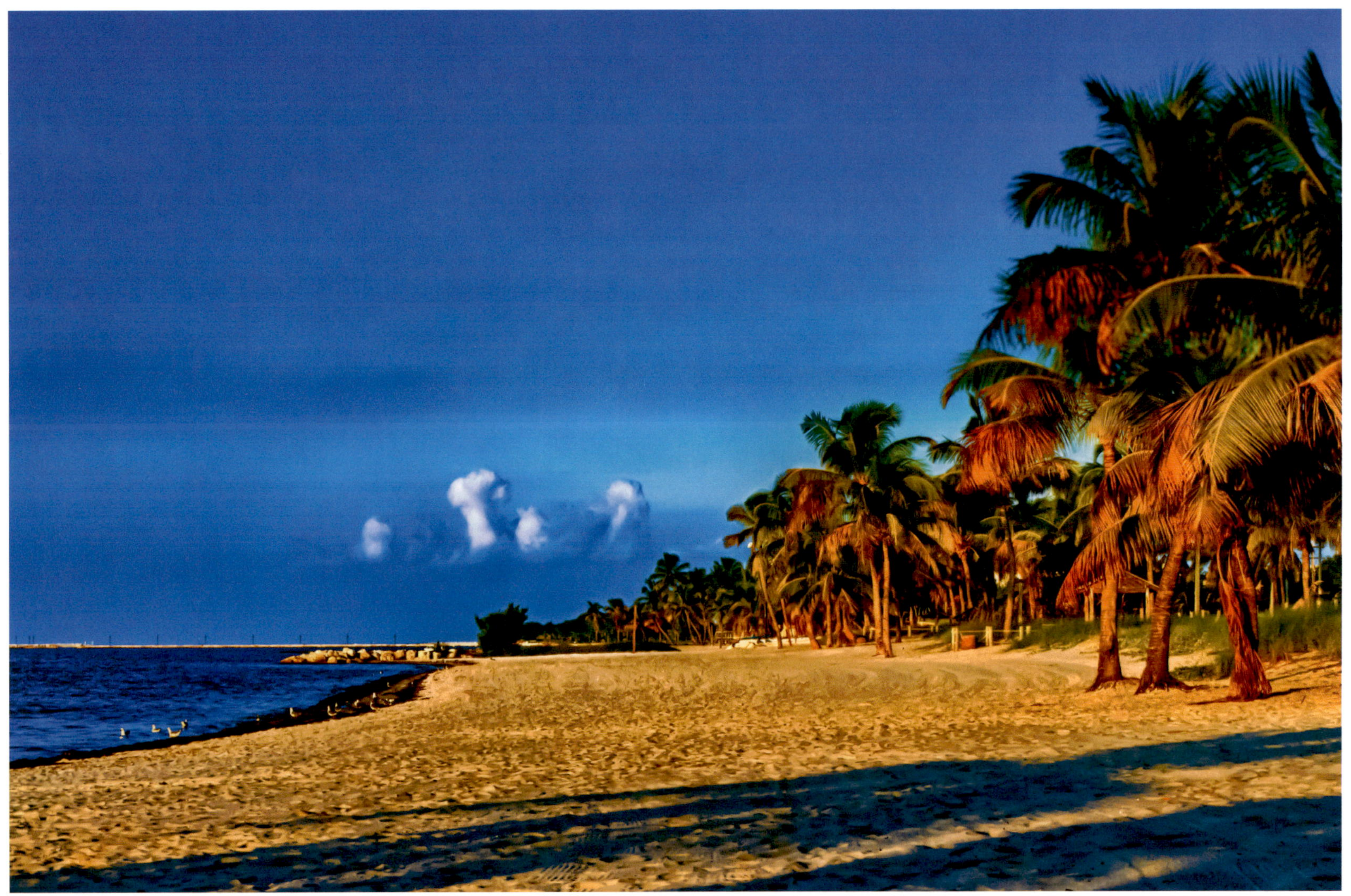

Smathers Beach: **V**ertical Clouds rise at Smathers Beach on the morning of October 11, 2011.

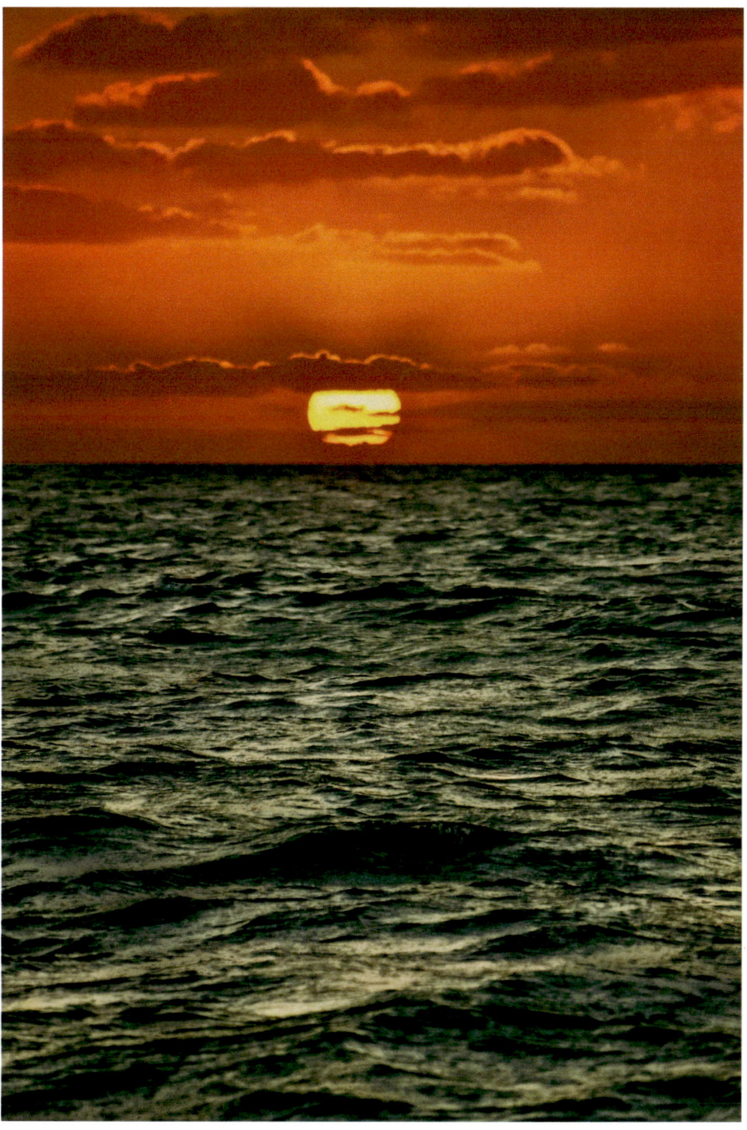

Stranded Sunrise: An extraordinary sunrise as I was stranded offshore of Big Pine, Florida on April 22, 2011.

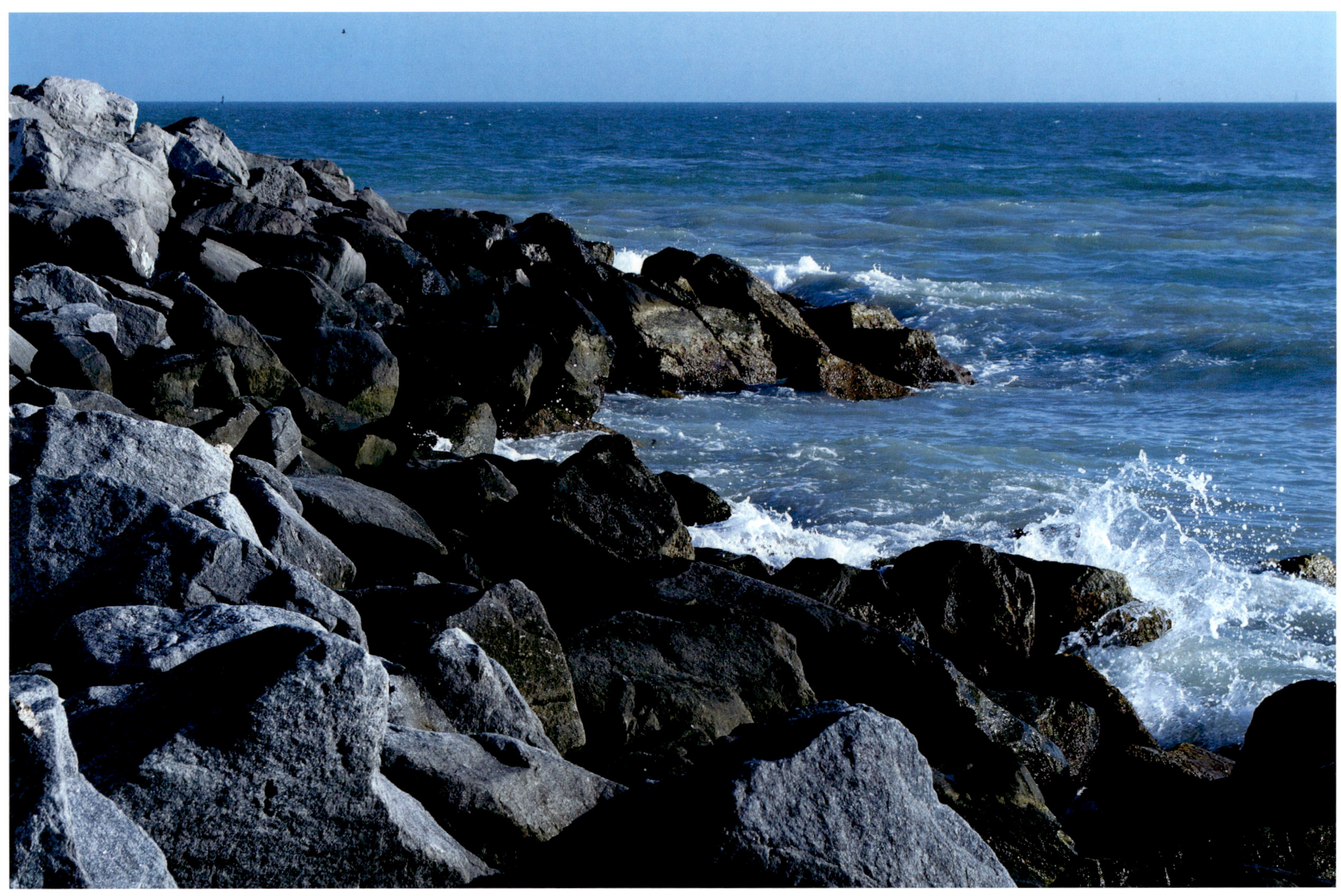

Ocean vs Rocks: Shot on June 26, 2010 at Fort Zachary Taylor State Park. Notice the rough texture of the rocks. They might be tough, but they'll probably loose this contest - eventually.

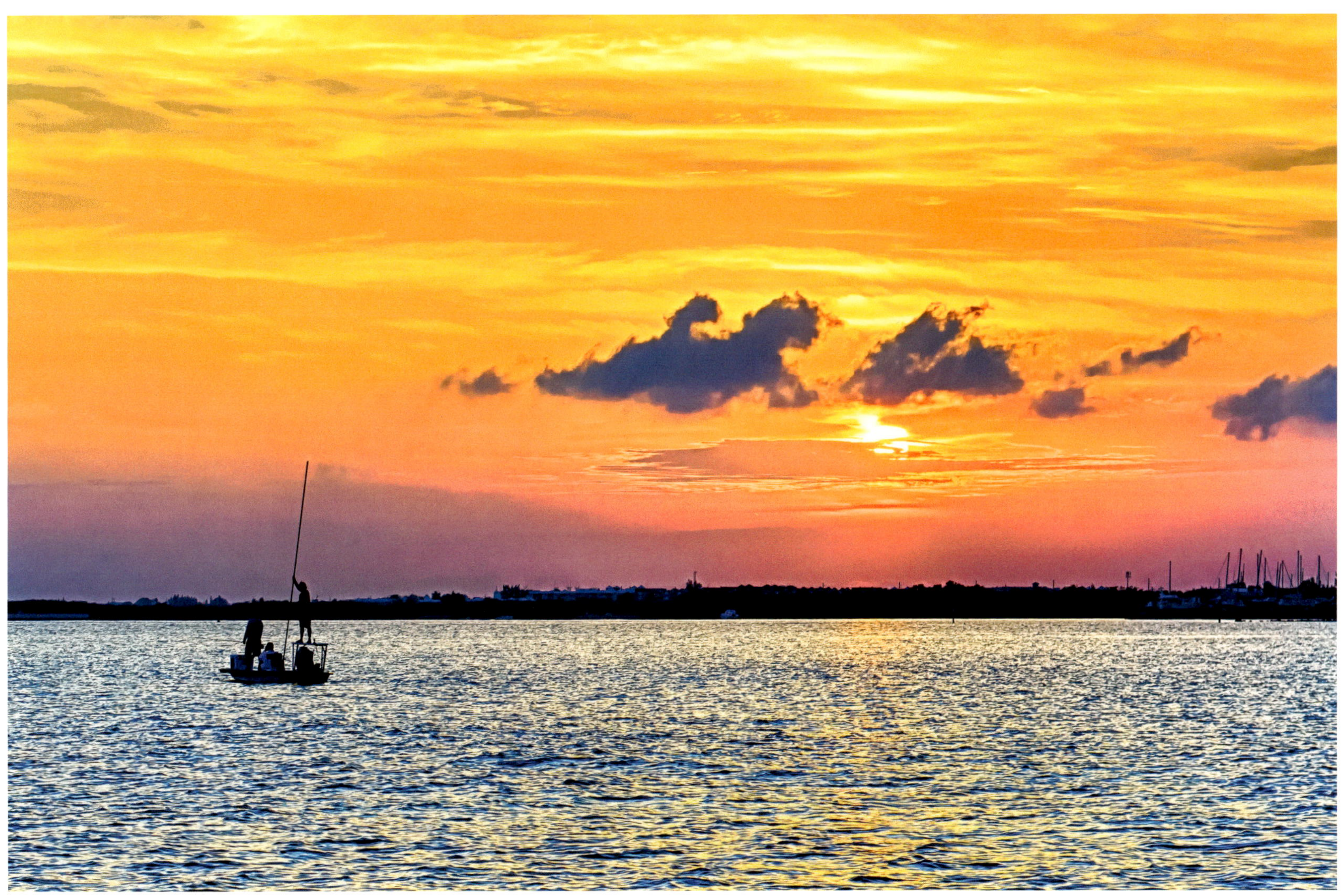

Flats Boat Sunset: An exquisite sunset on April 20, 2013 just offshore of Stock Island in the Florida Keys.

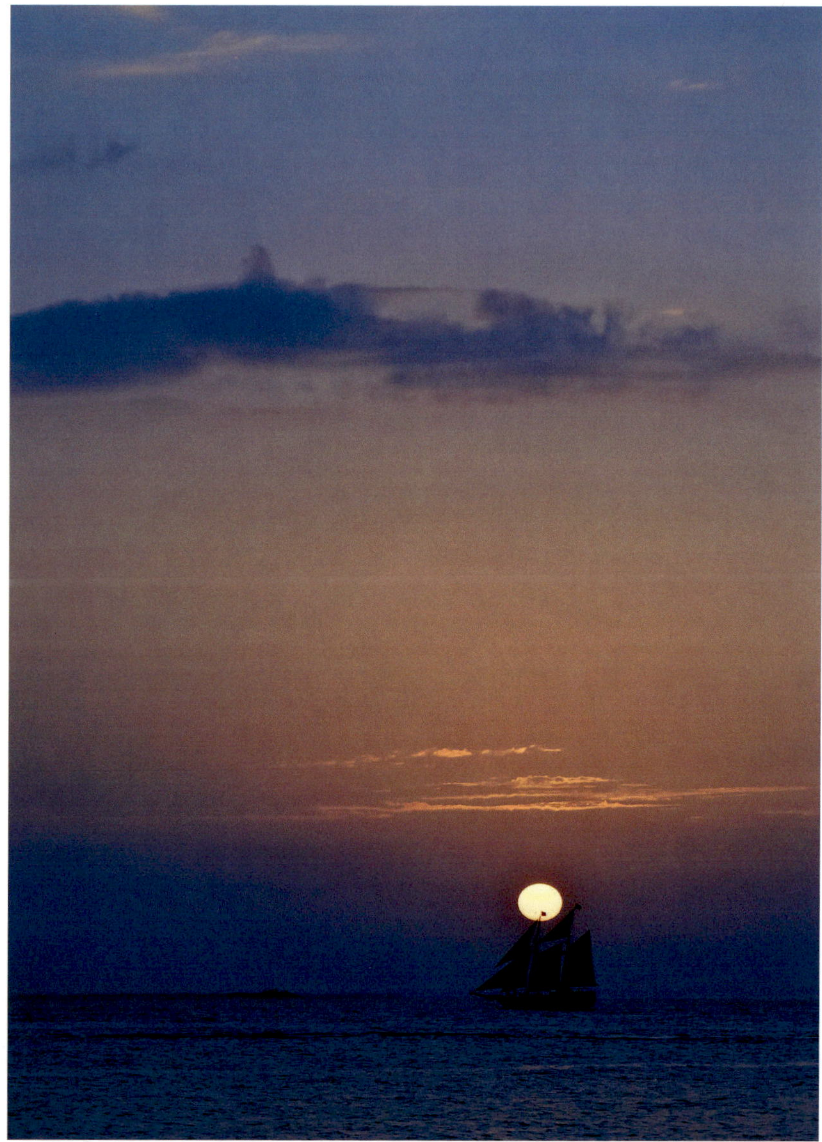

Blue Sunset: A schooner with topsails flying enjoys the Key West sunset.

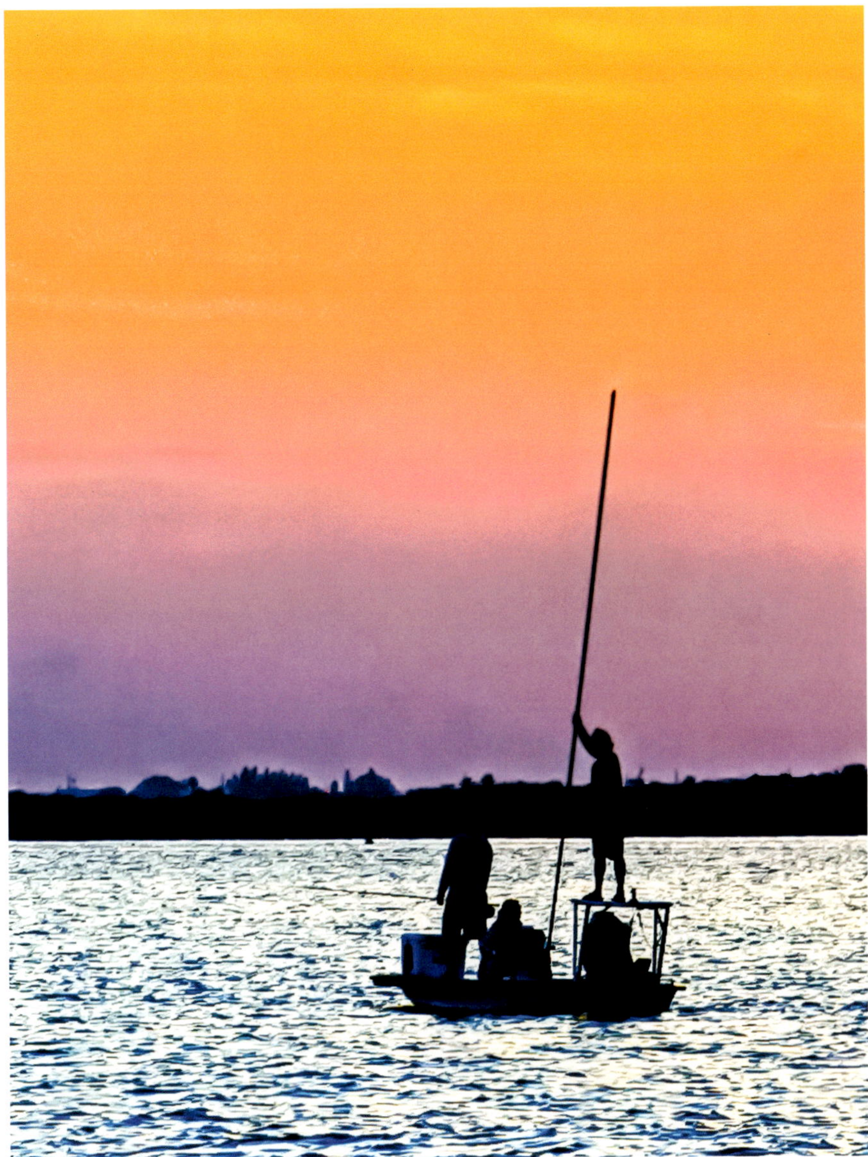

Flats Out: Flats boat fishing in the beautiful Florida Keys.

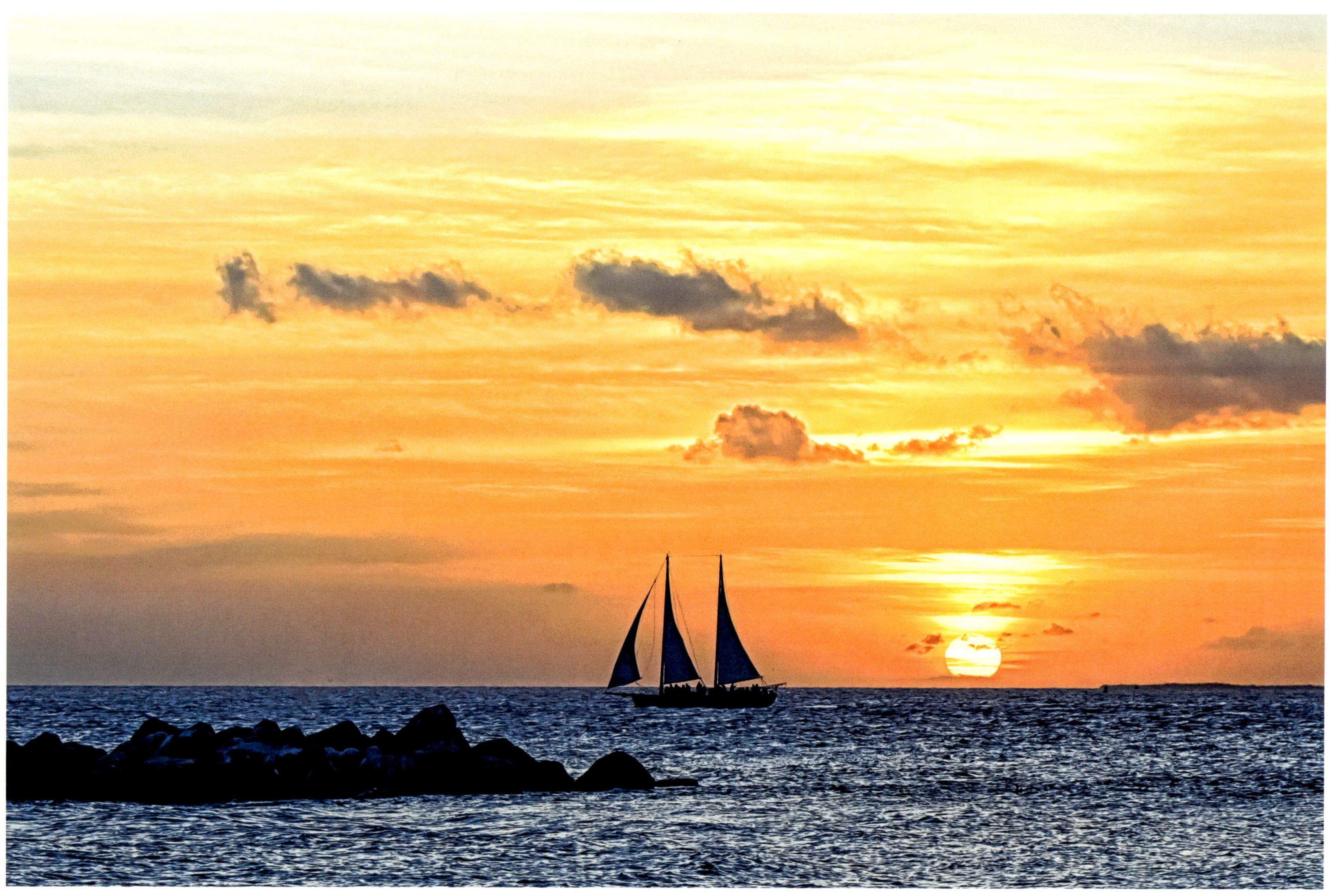

Serene Sunset Sail: A sailboat enjoys a splendid Key West sunset on February 21, 2012.

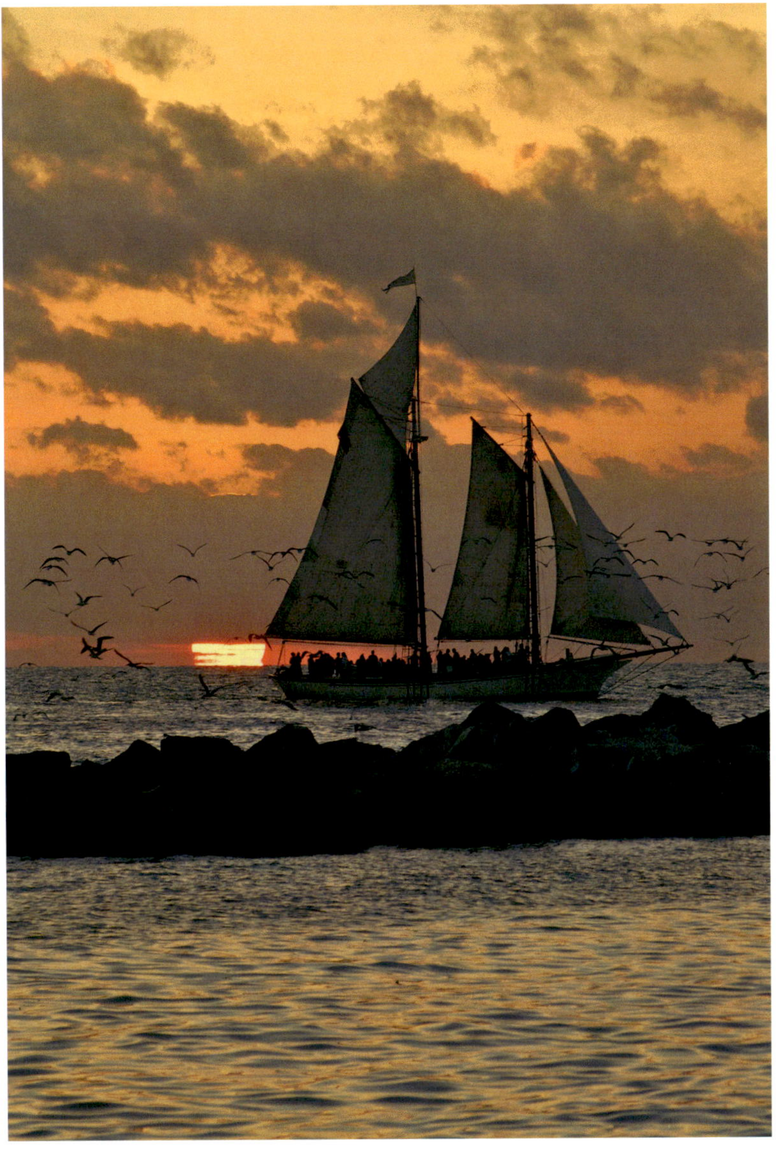

Sunset Flight: Birds take flight as the sun sets on January 7, 2011.

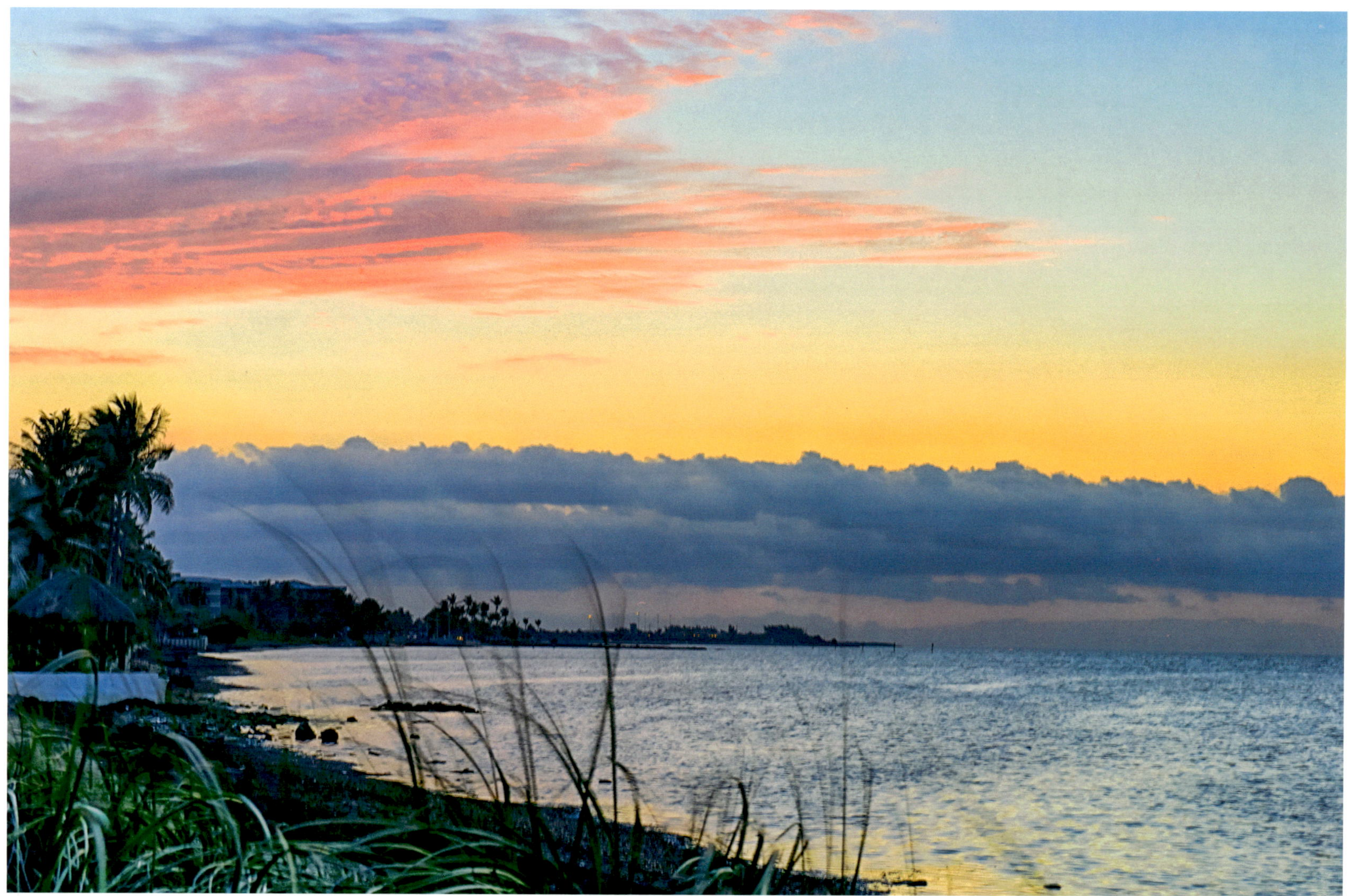

Key West Morning: A tranquil moment before sunrise at C.B. Harvey Park in Key West on March 31, 2013.

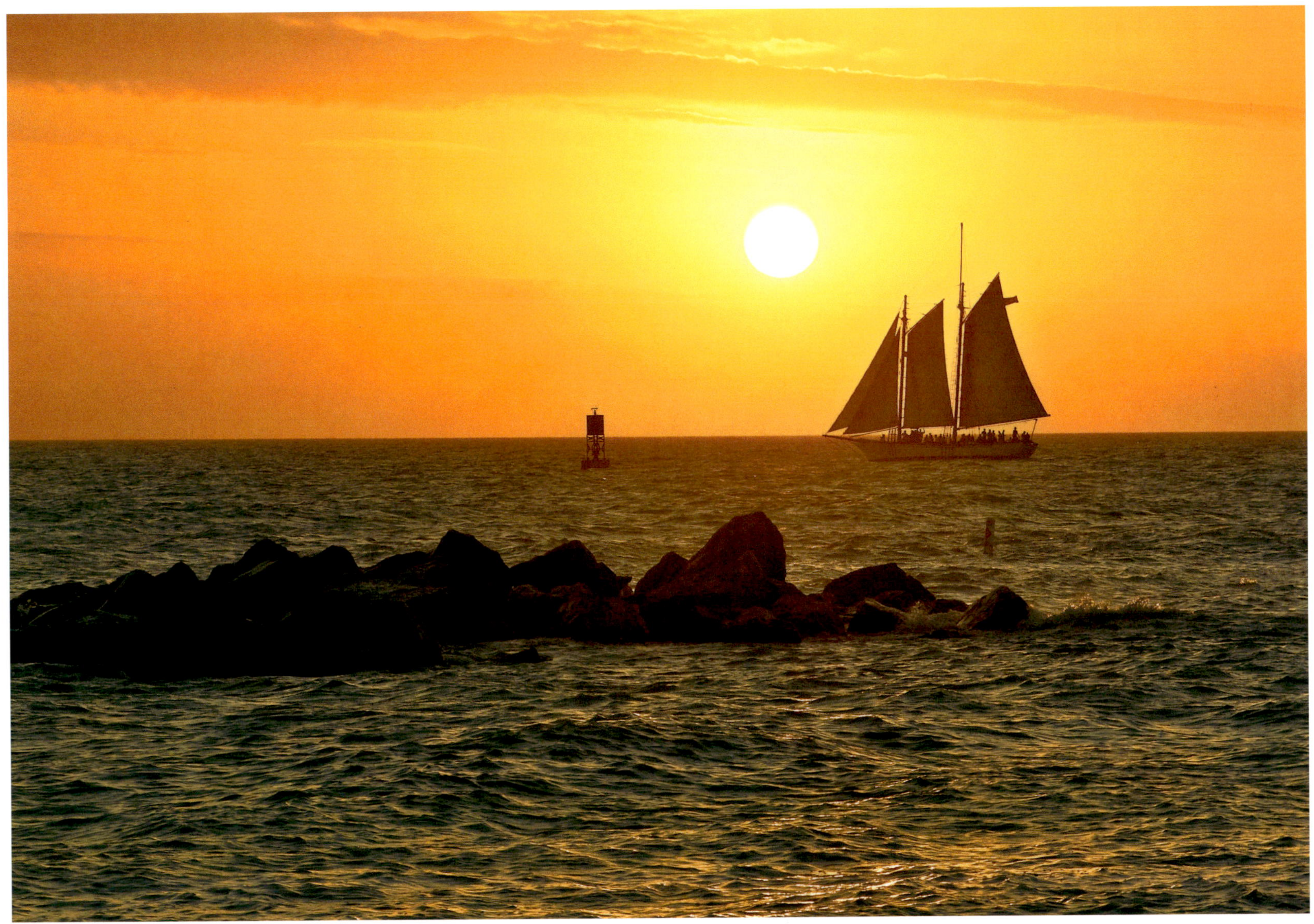

Feel the Heat: A full rigged schooner feels the heat of the Key West sun.

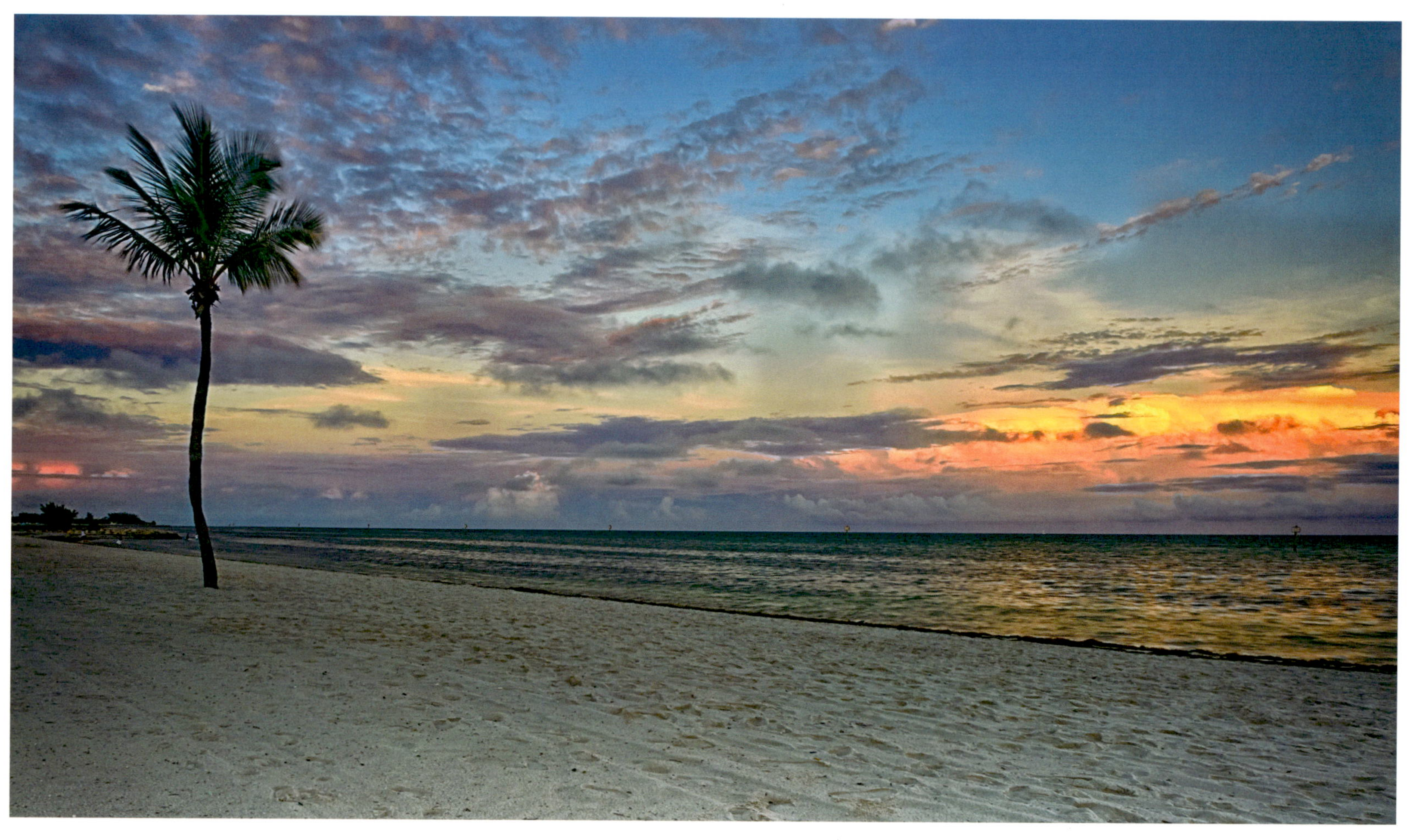

Smathers Beach Twilight: Looking east on Smathers Beach in Key West on the evening of May 29, 2013.

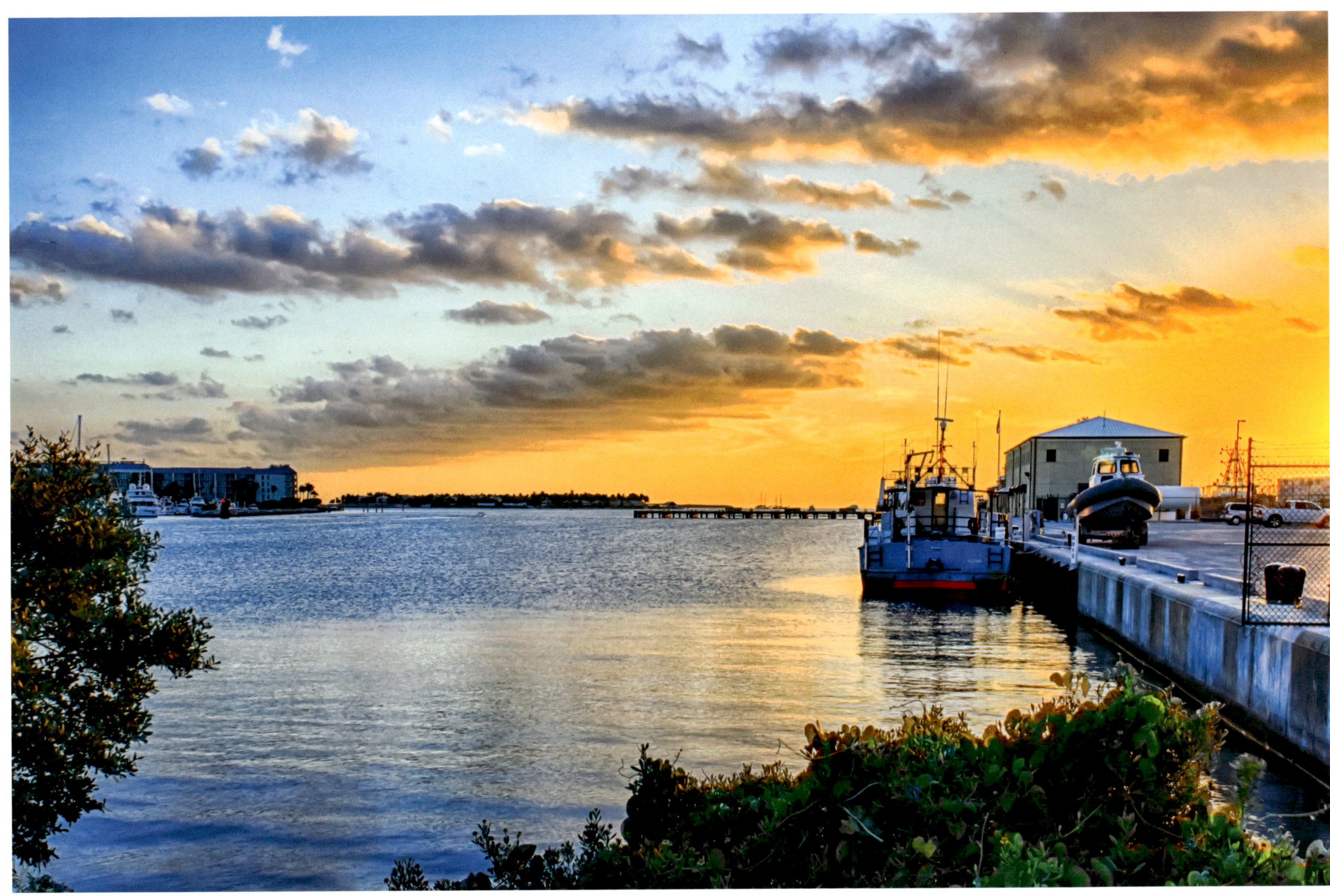

Trumbo Point Sunset: A beautiful sunset at Trumbo Point in Key West on June 12, 2012.

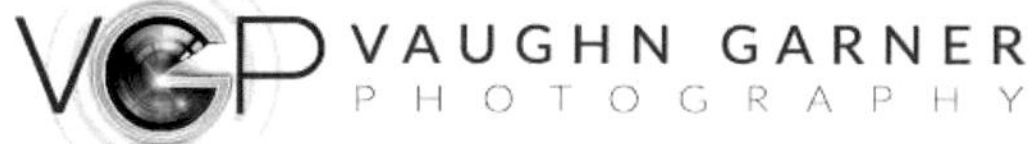

www.vaughngarnerphotography.com

Decorate your home and office with your favorite Fine Art Prints and Wall Art from Vaughn Garner Photography today! Visit www.vaughngarnerphotography.com, select an image from one of our galleries and click "Buy" for details.

Many different sizes are available from 8 x 12 inches up to 24 x 36 inches.

Paper: Choose a Finish for your Paper Print.

Lustre: Lustre is a premium finish on a heavier paper. It offers the vibrant colors of glossy with the fingerprint-resistant finish of matte. Printed on Kodak Supra Endura paper.

Glossy: Glossy is a shiny finish and prints appear brighter the Matte. Printed on Kodak paper.

Metallic: Rich, distinctive metallic look with a huge WOW! factor. Printed on Kodak Endura Professional Metallic paper.

Giclée Watercolor: Giclée process printing on premium fine art paper with a subtle texture. Finished with a protective spray.

Wall Art: Our Wall Art includes Traditional Canvas, Stretched Canvas, Flat Mounted Canvas, ThinWraps, and Metal.

Traditional Canvas: The canvas is wrapped around a wooden frame with part of the photo visible on the sides of the frame.

Stretched Canvas: The canvas is stretched around a wooden frame and stapled on the edges, leaving the full image visible on the front.

Flat Mounted Canvas: The canvas is mounted onto rigid Gatorboard.

ThinWraps: Wrapped around sturdy masonite board.

Metal: Durable, archival, and stunning.

Frames: We have 16 different styles of custom frames for your paper prints to choose from, and also offer several different mounting options including 3/4" Standout, Gatorfoam, and 2MM Styrene.

If you are not happy with the quality of your printed order, contact us within 30 days and we will reprint it free of charge.
Our goal is 100% customer satisfaction.